Estimation of Missing Water-Level Data for the Everglades Depth Estimation Network (EDEN)

By Paul A. Conrads and Matthew D. Petkewich

Prepared in cooperation with the
U.S. Geological Survey Greater Everglades Priority Ecosystems Science

Open-File Report 2009–1120

U.S. Department of the Interior
U.S. Geological Survey

U.S. Department of the Interior
KEN SALAZAR, Secretary

U.S. Geological Survey
Suzette M. Kimball, Acting Director

U.S. Geological Survey, Reston, Virginia: 2009

For more information on the USGS—the Federal source for science about the Earth, its natural and living resources, natural hazards, and the environment, visit *http://www.usgs.gov* or call 1-888-ASK-USGS

For an overview of USGS information products, including maps, imagery, and publications, visit *http://www.usgs.gov/pubprod*

To order this and other USGS information products, visit *http://store.usgs.gov*

Suggested citation:
Conrads, P.A., and Petkewich, M.D., 2009, Estimation of missing water-level data for the Everglades Depth Estimation Network (EDEN): U.S. Geological Survey Open-File Report 2009–1120, 53 p.

Preface

This report was originally released without a reference to the datum that data was stored in the National Water Information System (NWIS) database. The report has been revised with references to the datum for each station and the importance of using the correct datum to compute the correct estimation of water level.

Contents

Figures

Table

Conversion Factors

Multiply	By	To obtain
Length		
foot (ft)	0.3048	meter (m)
Area		
square foot (ft^2)	929.0	square centimeter (cm^2)
square foot (ft^2)	0.09290	square meter (m^2)
Flow Rate		
cubic foot per second (ft^3/s)	0.02832	cubic meter per second (m^3/s)

Acronyms and Abbreviations

BCNP	Big Cypress National Preserve
CERP	Comprehensive Everglades Restoration Plan
EDEN	Everglades Depth Estimation Network
ENP	Everglades National Park
GIS	geographic information system
ME	mean error
MSE	mean square error
NAVD 1988	North American Vertical Datum of 1988
NGVD 1929	National Geodetic Vertical Datum of 1929
NPS	National Park Service
NWIS	National Water Information System
OLS	ordinary least squares
P1	Predictor 1
P2	Predictor 2
P3	Predictor 3
P4	Predictor 4
PME	percent model error
R^2	coefficient of determination
RBF	radial basis function
RMSE	root mean square error
SFWMD	South Florida Water Management District
SOFIA	South Florida Information Access
USGS	U.S. Geological Survey
WCA	water conservation area
WL	water level

Estimation of Missing Water-Level Data for the Everglades Depth Estimation Network (EDEN)

By Paul A. Conrads and Matthew D. Petkewich

Abstract

The Everglades Depth Estimation Network (EDEN) is an integrated network of real-time water-level gaging stations, ground-elevation models, and water-surface elevation models designed to provide scientists, engineers, and water-resource managers with current (2000–2009) water-depth information for the entire freshwater portion of the greater Everglades. The U.S. Geological Survey Greater Everglades Priority Ecosystems Science provides support for EDEN and their goal of providing quality-assured monitoring data for the U.S. Army Corps of Engineers Comprehensive Everglades Restoration Plan. To increase the accuracy of the daily water-surface elevation model, water-level estimation equations were developed to fill missing data. To minimize the occurrences of no estimation of data due to missing data for an input station, a minimum of three linear regression equations were developed for each station using different input stations. Of the 726 water-level estimation equations developed to fill missing data at 239 stations, more than 60 percent of the equations have coefficients of determination greater than 0.90, and 92 percent have an coefficient of determination greater than 0.70.

Introduction

The Everglades Depth Estimation Network (EDEN) is an integrated network of real-time water-level gaging stations, ground-elevation models, and water-surface elevation models designed to provide scientists, engineers, and water-resource managers with current (2000–2009) water-depth information for the entire freshwater portion of the greater Everglades (Telis, 2005, 2006). EDEN is presented on a 400-square-meter (m^2) grid, and EDEN offers a consistent and documented dataset that can be used by scientists and managers to (1) guide large-scale field operations, (2) integrate hydrologic and ecological responses, and (3) support biological and ecological assessments that measure ecosystem responses to the Comprehensive Everglades Restoration Plan (CERP; U.S. Army Corps of Engineers, 1999). The target users of EDEN are biologists and ecologists who can use the information to examine trophic-level responses to hydrodynamic changes in the Everglades. The EDEN database is a 9-year dataset of baseline conditions prior to the implementation of the CERP and offers investigators a single repository for historic hourly water-level data.

To estimate water depths in the greater Everglades, geographic information system (GIS) models have been developed to determine the ground elevation and water-surface elevation for the freshwater portion of the Everglades. The water-depth estimates are the differences between the two surfaces. Data to support the ground-elevation model include elevation measurements at more than 50,000 sites (Desmond, 2003). Data to support the water-surface model include continuous water levels at 256 stations (fig. 1), including 25 stations that were added to the EDEN database in 2006. The water levels for the 25 recently added stations were hindcasted to 2000 to be concurrent with the other stations in the EDEN database (Conrads and Roehl, 2007).

For the development of the ground-elevation model (Jones and Price, 2007), the EDEN domain was divided into a large number of equal-sized 400-m^2 cells that in total are referred to as the "grid." The grid includes information on the characteristics of each cell, such as centroid location, the area of the Everglades it represents, average elevation, and percentage of the vegetation type (slough, prairie, sawgrass, upland, exotic, and other). The large number of highly accurate elevation data allowed for further refinement of the ground-elevation model. The geostatistical technique of kriging was selected for the EDEN ground-elevation model following extensive testing of multiple interpolation techniques. Kriging produced the lowest average error for validating elevation points and provides useful diagnostic surfaces. To account for variations within subregions of the EDEN area, individual geostatistical models were created for each water conservation area (WCA), the Everglades National Park (ENP), and portions of Big Cypress National Preserve (BCNP). These individual models were combined to create a single, 400-m^2-resolution ground-elevation model for the entire EDEN domain (fig. 2).

A water-surface elevation model for the freshwater portion of the EDEN domain was developed in a GIS using the EDEN grid described above. The EDEN water-surface model interpolates measured daily water levels from 239 stations in the EDEN continuous monitoring network to ungaged

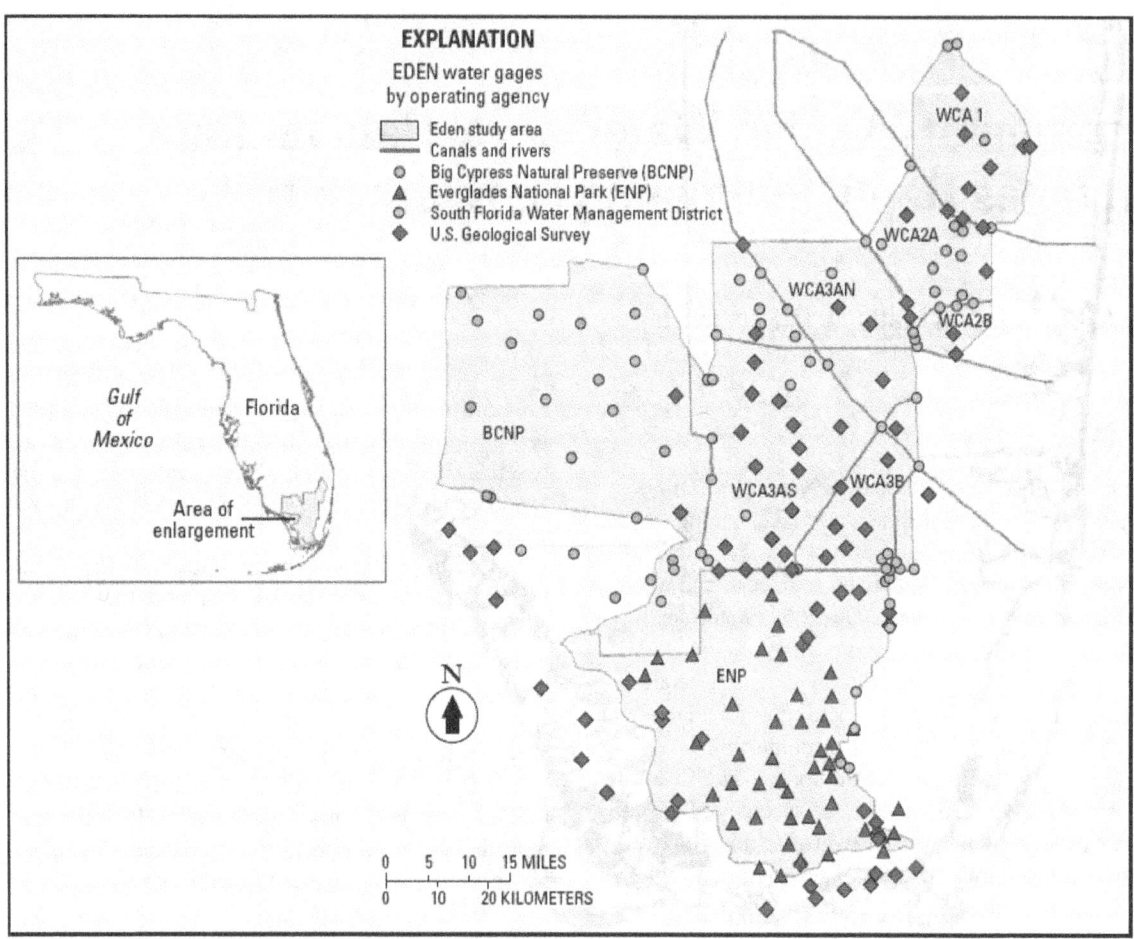

Figure 1. Location of water-level gages in Everglades Depth Estimation Network (EDEN). Water Conservation Areas (WCA) 2 and 3 are subdivided by canals. WCA3A is further subdivided into a northern (WCA3AN) and a southern (WCA3AS) region (from Pearlstine and others, 2007).

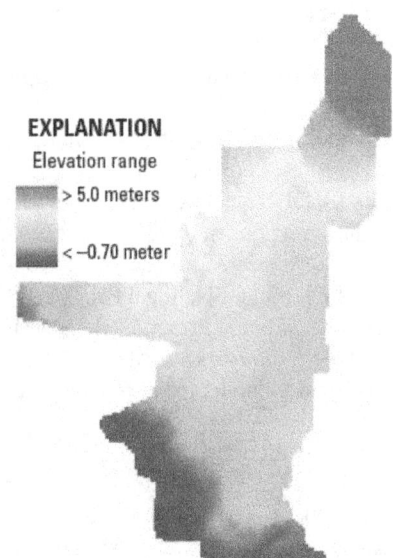

Figure 2. Everglades Depth Estimation Network (EDEN) digital elevation model released in January 2007 (from Jones and Price, 2007).

locations using radial basis functions (RBF) with multiquadric regression (Pearlstine and others, 2007; Palaseanu and Pearlstine, 2008). The model produces a continuous water surface for any day within the period of record in the EDEN database. An example of the water surface for two sample days is shown in figure 3.

Often, data may be missing because of instrumentation or transmission problems for the 239-station network used to model the water surface of the freshwater portion of the Everglades. In addition, 25 stations currently (January 2009) do not have telemetry for real-time transmission of data. When data from a particular station are missing, the water-surface model does not use that station for generating the water-surface map for that day. Depending on the number of stations with missing data and the location, the quality of the water-surface maps can be diminished by missing data. To increase the accuracy of the daily water surface, water-level estimation equations were developed to fill missing data. For each station, at least three linear regression equations were developed to estimate missing data for the station. This report presents the development of the equations and summarizes their performance statistics.

Data-Collection Network

The EDEN database is composed of hourly water-level data from 256 gaging stations (239 stations in the freshwater portion of the Everglades) and includes marsh and river stations (appendix 1) and canal stations (appendix 2) operated by the BCNP, ENP, the South Florida Water Management District (SFWMD), and the U.S. Geological Survey (USGS). In this report, the names of the EDEN stations follow the naming convention used by EDEN (*http://sofia.usgs.gov/eden/ explanation.php#stationname*) and are generally similar to the names used by the agency that maintains the gage. The

datasets with the estimated missing record are available on the EDEN Web page on the South Florida Information Access (SOFIA) Web site—*http://sofia.usgs.gov/eden/index.php*.

Estimation of Water-Level Data

The following procedure was used to develop estimation equations of water-level data for the 239 stations used to generate the surface-water maps:

- A cross-correlation matrix of all the stations was generated using the daily values of the period of record of the EDEN database. For each station, the highest correlated stations were determined and used for input to the estimation equations.

- To minimize the inability to estimate data due to missing data from an input station, three equations were developed for each station using different input stations. For selected stations, a fourth equation was developed to further minimize the occurrence of missing estimations.

- Linear regression equations were generated by determining the slope and y-intercept for each station relative to the input stations. For each station, a priority was established for the order of the regression equations to be used to fill a data gap. The order that the equations will be used was based on performance statistics, visual inspection of equation predictions and measured data, and proximity of input and output stations.

- A Microsoft Access® database of the EDEN water-level data and estimation equations was developed to automate the filling of missing data. A log file is generated that documents which input station was used to fill missing water-level data for each station.

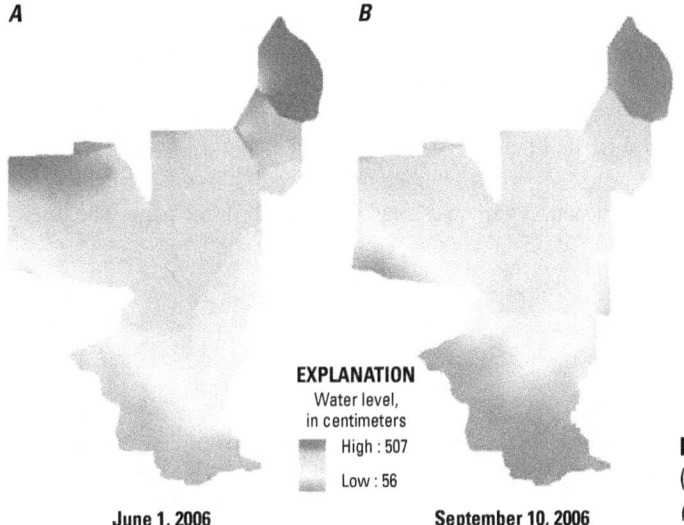

Figure 3. Example of Everglades Depth Estimation Network (EDEN) water-surface map for *(A)* a wet season day and *(B)* a dry season day (from Pearlstine and others, 2007).

The equations are in the form of $y = mx + b$, where y is the estimated value, m is the slope, x is the value from the input station, and b is the y-intercept. The equations were developed using 8 years of daily data and can be used to estimate either daily or hourly values. The EDEN water-surface elevation model uses daily median values to minimize the influence of outliers in the real-time data.

The estimation of missing data is computed after the data is retrieved from NWIS and prior to pre-processing the data to generate daily water-level surfaces. The water-level data for a majority of stations in the National Water Information System (NWIS) are stored to North American Vertical Datum of 1988 (NAVD 1988). For the stations with water levels stored to National Geodetic Vertical Datum of 1929 (NGVD 1929), the data preprocessing program converts the water-level data to NAVD 1988. The estimation equations use the datum used in the retrieval from NWIS, and the datums of the stations are listed in appendixes 1 and 2.

The 726 water-level estimation equations are presented in appendix 3. The stations are listed in numerical and alphabetical order. For each station, the three or four estimation equations are listed (Predictors—P1, P2, P3, and P4) with the values for the slope and y-intercept. Statistical measures of prediction accuracy for the estimation equations also are listed. The goodness-of-fit statistics presented in appendix 3 for the equations are the Pearson correlation coefficient (R), coefficient of determination (R^2), mean error (ME), root mean square error (RMSE), standard error, relative bias (ME divided by the average measured value, in percent), percent model error (PME, computed as the RMSE divided by the range of the measured data), and Nash-Sutcliffe efficiency index. The order of the estimation equations generally was based on the overall goodness-of-fit represented by R^2 and RMSE. The location of the station and input stations ("predictors") also are listed in appendix 3.

Each statistic measures a different aspect of the accuracy of the prediction equations. Estimation accuracy commonly is reported in terms of R^2 and is interpreted as the goodness-of-fit of an equation or model. A second interpretation may answer the question, "How much information does one variable or a group of variables provide about the behavior of another variable?" In the first context, an $R^2 = 0.6$ might be disappointing, whereas in the latter, it is merely an accounting of how much information is shared by the variables being used.

The standard error is the measure of the scatter of the actual observations about the regression line and is the standard deviation of the error of the predicted values in the regression. The standard error can be used to compute confidence intervals for the predictions. The relative bias is the ratio of the mean error to the average measured values.

The ME and RMSE statistics provide a measure of the prediction accuracy of the estimation equations. The ME is a measure of the bias of model predictions—whether the model over- or underpredicts the measured data. The ME is presented as the adjustment of the estimated values to equal the measured values; therefore, positive and negative MEs indicate an over- or underprediction bias by the model, respectively. MEs near zero may be misleading because negative and positive discrepancies in the simulations can cancel each other. RMSEs address the limitations of ME by computing the magnitude, rather than the direction (sign) of the discrepancies. The units of the ME and RMSE statistics are the same as the variable simulated by the model. Some find the bias of the model, or ME, easier to interpret when presented in relative terms. The relative bias is computed by dividing the ME by the mean of the measured values.

The accuracy of the models, as given by RMSE, should be evaluated with respect to the range of the output variable. A model may have a low RMSE, but if the range of the output variable is small, the model may only be accurate for a limited range of conditions and the model error may be a relatively large percentage of the model response. Likewise, a model may have a large RMSE, but if the range of the output variable is large, the model error may be a relatively small percentage of the total model response. The PME is computed by dividing the RMSE by the range of the measured data.

To address the limitation of R^2, Nash and Sutcliffe (1970) developed an efficiency index to evaluate the goodness-of-fit of hydrologic models. The Nash-Sutcliffe efficiency index can range from $-\infty$ to 1. An efficiency of 1 corresponds to a perfect match of simulated streamflow to the observed data. An efficiency of 0 indicates that the model predictions are as accurate as the mean of the observed data used to develop the model, whereas an efficiency index less than 0 occurs when the observed mean is a better predictor than the model. In summary, models with an efficiency index from 0 to 1 provide a better estimate than the mean of the observed data, and the higher the value, the better the estimates. Models with an index of 1 match the observed data perfectly, and for models with an index of less than 1, the mean of the observed data provides a better estimate. McCuen and others (2006) noted that only subjective evaluations of the efficiency index was possible and that the index is influenced by sample size, model bias, timing errors, and outliers.

The following is an example of how to use appendix 3. Find the station of interest, for example S146_H, a marsh structure in Water Conservation Area 2A (appendix 1). The three input stations, or predictors, are S144_H, S145_H, and S11A_H and are listed as P1, P2, and P3, respectively. Make sure that the data for the predictor stations are for the datum used for the gage (appendixes 1 and 2). The water-level estimation will be for the datum used for the gage. The three estimation equations are:

P1: $Y_{estimated} = 1.02(X_{S144\_H}) - 0.58$,

P2: $Y_{estimated} = 0.99(X_{S145\_H}) - 0.37$, and

P3: $Y_{estimated} = 1.02(X_{S11A\_H}) - 2.34$.

The $Y_{estimated}$ station is S146_H, and X is the input (predictor) station. If the data for S146_H are missing, the first predictor station, S144_H, is used to estimate the data. In the event that the data for S144_H also are missing, then S145_H is used as the input station (P2). In the event that the data for both

S144_H and S145_H are missing, then the data for S11A_H are used as the input station (P3). As stated earlier, in some instances a fourth station is necessary when the first three input stations are missing data for the same period of time.

The R²s for the three estimation equations are 0.99, 0.98, and 0.95, respectively, and the MEs are 0.04, 0.03, and 0.04 foot (ft), respectively. The RMSE for the equations range from 0.16 to 0.25 ft, and the relative biases for the three equations are 0.4, 0.3, and 0.4 percent, respectively. The Nash-Sutcliffe efficiency index was 0.97 for P1 and P2 and was 0.93 for P3. Overall, the percent model error for the predictor equations is less than 5 percent. All three predictor stations are located in Water Conservation Area 2A. The measured and estimated water levels for station S146_H are shown in figure 4.

The majority of the water-level estimation equations provide good estimates for missing values. Figure 5A shows the sorted histogram of the frequency and cumulative percents of the R²s for the 239 first predictor estimation equations. Ninety-eight percent of the equations (234) have R²s greater than 0.70, and 2 percent (5 equations) have R²s less than 0.70. The frequency and cumulative percentages for all 726 equations are shown in figure 5B. More than 60 percent of the equations

have R²s greater than 0.95, and more than 95 percent have R²s greater than 0.70. The minimum, median, and maximum values of the summary statistics for all 726 equations are shown in table 1. Caution should be used when using equations with particularly poor performance statistics.

Table 1. Minimum, median, and maximum values for the summary statistics for the 726 estimation equations.

[R², coefficient of determination; RMSE, root mean square error]

Statistic	Minimum	Median	Maximum
R²	0.01	0.94	1.00
Mean error	−0.19	0.00	0.25
RMSE	0.02	0.17	1.24
Standard error	0.02	0.16	1.04
Nash-Sutcliffe	0.01	0.94	1.00
Percent model error	0.4%	4.7%	21.1%
Percent model bias	−38.3%	0.0%	32.3%

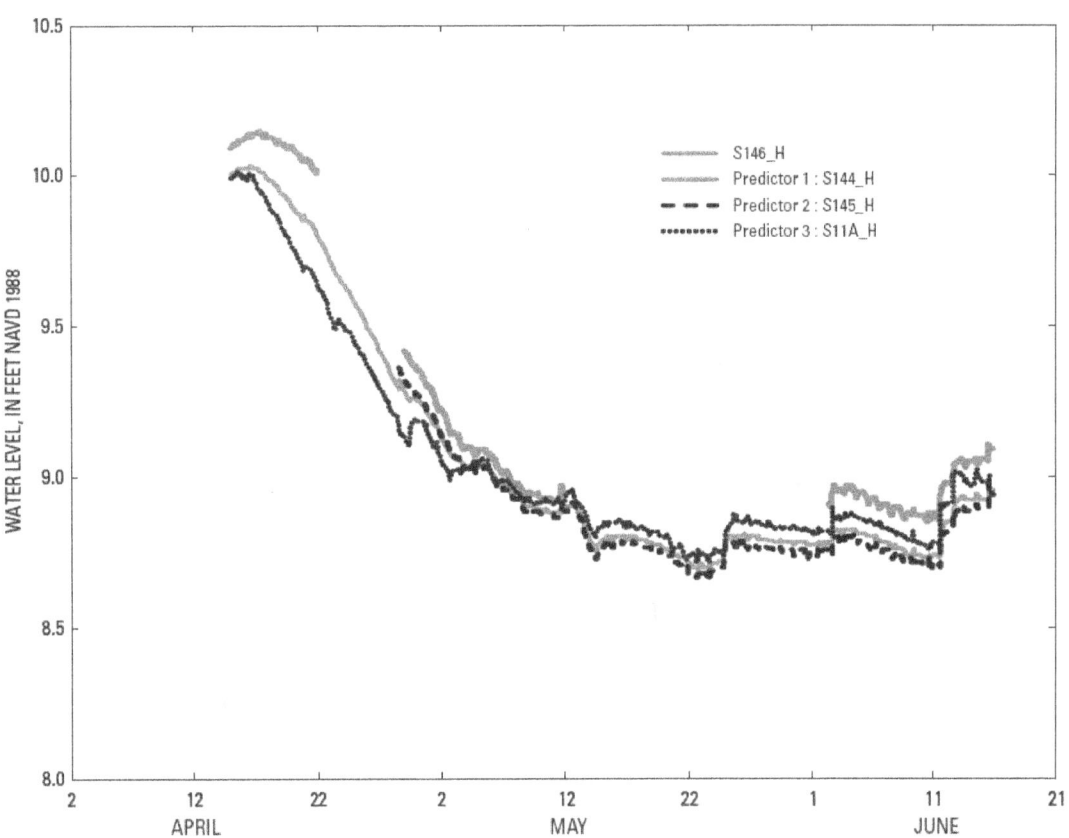

Figure 4. Measured and estimated water level for station S146_H using three input (predictor) stations for the period April 15, 2008, to June 15, 2008. Water levels for stations S146_H, S144_H, and S145_H are in NAVD 1988, and water levels for station S11A_H are in NGVD 1929 (appendix 1). All the estimates for S146_H are in NAVD 1988.

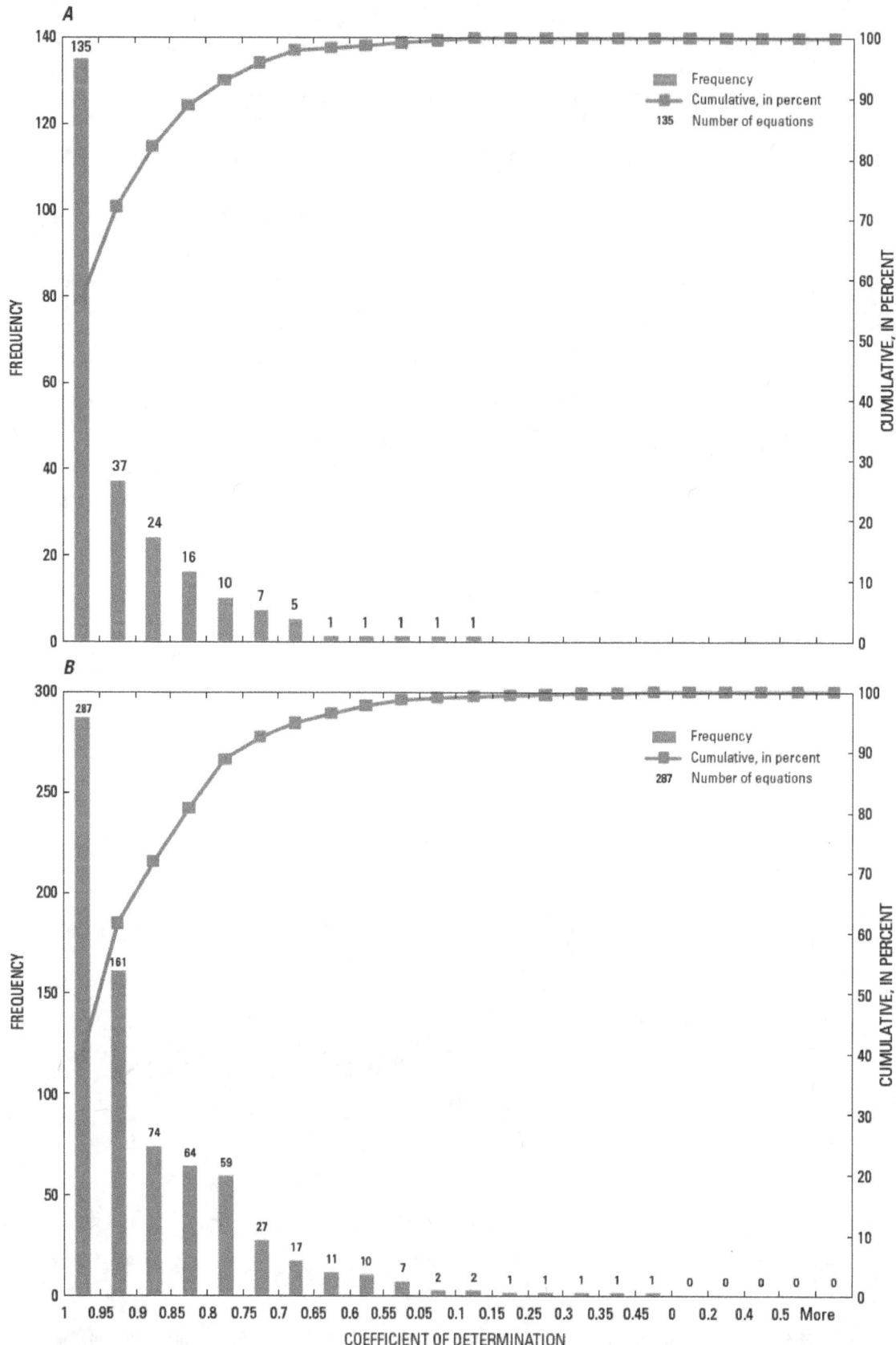

Figure 5.   Sorted frequency histograms and cumulative percentages of coefficients of determination (R²) of (A) the 239 first predictor (P1) water-level estimation equations and (B) all 726 water-level estimation equations.

Summary and Discussion

The Everglades Depth Estimation Network (EDEN) is an integrated network of real-time water-level gaging stations, ground-elevation models, and water-surface elevation models. The network provides scientists, engineers, and water-resource managers with current (2000–2009) water-depth information for the entire freshwater portion of the greater Everglades. A spatially-continuous interpolated water surface across the greater Everglades is generated from daily median water-level values. Missing or erroneous data diminish the quality of the modeled water surfaces. To increase the accuracy of the daily water-surface model, an application was developed to estimate water levels to fill data gaps. Missing data were estimated by developing linear regression equations for each site. To minimize the inability to estimate data due to missing data from an input site, three or four regression equations were developed for each site using different input sites. For each site, an order was established for the regression equation to be used to fill a data gap. The 726 equations were incorporated into a database application that automatically estimates missing records. The performance statistics computed for each equation provides documentation of the goodness-of-fit of the equations. In addition, although the majority of the equations provide satisfactory estimations of water levels, the performance statistic provides a prioritization for identifying stations where improved equations are needed to provide more satisfactory water-level estimates.

Acknowledgments

The complexity of this study required interagency cooperation in addition to individual contributions. The authors thank the members of the EDEN project team: Aaron Higer and Zhongwei Lui from the University of Florida, and Heather Henkel, Michael Holmes, Dr. John W. Jones, Carolyn Price, and Pamela Telis of the USGS. The authors also thank the funding agencies that support the EDEN project team—U.S. Army Corps of Engineers, Jacksonville District, and the USGS Greater Everglades Priority Ecosystems Science.

References Cited

Conrads, P.A., and Roehl, E.A., Jr., 2007, Hydrologic record extension of water-level data in the Everglades Depth Estimation Network (EDEN) using artificial neural network models, 2000–2006: U.S. Geological Survey Open-File Report 2007–1350, 56 p.

Desmond, G.D., 2003, Measuring and mapping the topography of the Florida Everglades for Ecosystem Restoration: U.S. Geological Survey Fact Sheet 021–03, 4 p.

Jones, J.W., and Price, S.D., 2007, Everglades Depth Estimation Network (EDEN) digital elevation model research and development: U.S. Geological Survey Open-File Report 2007–1034, 29 p.

McCuen, R.H., Knight, Zachary, and Cutter, A.G., 2006, Evaluation of the Nash-Sutcliffe Efficiency Index: Journal of Hydrologic Engineers, v. 11, no. 6, p. 597–602.

Nash, J.E., and Sutcliffe, J.V., 1970, River flow forecasting through conceptual models, Part 1—A discussion of principles: Journal of Hydrology, v. 10, no. 3, p. 282–290.

Palaseanu, M., and Pearlstine, L., 2008, Estimation of water surface elevations for the Everglades, Florida: Computers and Geosciences, doi:10.1016/j.cageo.2007.08.004.

Pearlstine, L., Higer, A., Palaseanu, M., Fujisaki, I., and Mazzotti, F., 2007, Spatially continuous interpolation of water stage and water depths using the Everglades Depth Estimation Network (EDEN): Gainesville, FL, Institute of Food and Agriculture, University of Florida, CIR1521, 18 p., 2 apps.

Telis, P.A., 2005, Project description, South Florida Surface Water Monitoring Network for the Support of MAP Projects (known as EDEN, Everglades Depth Estimation Network), accessed October 2, 2007, at *http://sofia.usgs.gov/projects/eden/*

Telis, P.A., 2006, The Everglades Depth Estimation Network (EDEN) for support of ecological and biological assessments: U.S. Geological Survey Fact Sheet 2006–3087, 4 p.

U.S. Army Corps of Engineers, 1999, Central and southern Florida project, comprehensive review study—Final integrated feasibility report and programmatic environmental impact statement: Jacksonville, FL, variously paged, 4 annexes, 15 apps.

Volin, J., Liu, Z., Higer, A., Mazzotti, F., Owen, D., Allen, J., and Pearlstine, L., 2008, Validation of a spatially continuous EDEN water-surface model for the Everglades, Florida: Department of Natural Resources Management and Engineering, University of Connecticut, 55 p.

Appendixes

Appendix 1.   EDEN marsh stations, type of station, operating agency, location, and real-time status sorted by location (from Volin and others, 2008).

[NWIS, National Water Information System; UTM, Universal Transverse Mercator; NAVD 1988, North American Vertical Datum of 1988; NGVD 1929, National Geodetic Vertical Datum of 1929; BCNP, Big Cypress National Preserve; SFWMD, South Florida Water Management District; USGS, U.S. Geological Survey; ENP, Everglades National Park; , degrees; ′, minutes; ″, seconds]

Station name	Datum of data stored in NWIS	Type of station	Operating agency	Latitude	Longitude	UTM Easting	UTM Northing	Daily real-time data available?
Big Cypress National Preserve								
BCA1	NAVD 1988	Marsh	BCNP	26°14′33″	81°19′14″	467985.60	2902579.23	Yes
BCA10	NAVD 1988	Marsh	BCNP	25°42′49″	81°01′19″	497798.55	2843968.89	Yes
BCA11	NAVD 1988	Marsh	BCNP	25°47′21″	81°06′00″	489974.43	2852339.53	Yes
BCA12	NAVD 1988	Marsh	BCNP	26°11′29″	81°05′12″	491340.70	2896882.12	Yes
BCA13	NAVD 1988	Marsh	BCNP	26°05′35″	81°03′13″	494638.96	2885990.32	Yes
BCA14	NAVD 1988	Marsh	BCNP	26°02′40″	81°18′00″	469987.92	2880640.29	Yes
BCA15	NAVD 1988	Marsh	SFWMD	26°02′23″	81°01′36″	497332.16	2880083.11	Yes
BCA16	NAVD 1988	Marsh	SFWMD	26°03′24″	81°09′20″	484439.83	2881968.62	Yes
BCA17	NAVD 1988	Marsh	SFWMD	26°12′18″	81°10′05″	483210.67	2898397.49	Yes
BCA18	NAVD 1988	Marsh	SFWMD	26°12′24″	80°58′59″	501692.78	2898571.30	Yes
BCA19	NAVD 1988	Marsh	SFWMD	25°47′35″	81°12′08″	479726.72	2852781.94	Yes
BCA2	NAVD 1988	Marsh	BCNP	26°11′46″	81°17′19″	471164.52	2897434.26	Yes
BCA20	NAVD 1988	Marsh	SFWMD	25°42′23″	80°56′05″	506549.00	2843170.54	Yes
BCA3	NAVD 1988	Marsh	BCNP	26°09′24″	81°13′18″	477845.59	2893052.76	Yes
BCA4	NAVD 1988	Marsh	BCNP	25°57′26″	81°06′14″	489599.28	2870950.61	Yes
BCA5	NAVD 1988	Marsh	BCNP	25°58′06″	80°55′35″	507368.80	2872179.04	Yes
BCA6	NAVD 1988	Marsh	BCNP	25°51′07″	80°58′52″	501892.72	2859287.93	Yes
BCA7	NAVD 1988	Marsh	BCNP	25°53′12″	81°15′44″	473732.23	2863159.23	Yes
BCA8	NAVD 1988	Marsh	BCNP	25°53′25″	81°16′13″	472926.09	2863560.77	Yes
BCA9	NAVD 1988	Marsh	BCNP	25°46′42″	80°54′44″	508801.02	2851138.96	Yes
EDEN_1	NAVD 1988	Marsh	USGS	25°51′38″	80°53′42″	510520.53	2860245.60	Yes
EDEN_6	NAVD 1988	Marsh	USGS	26°03′55″	80°54′14″	509613.26	2882916.52	Yes
L28_GAP	NAVD 1988	Marsh	SFWMD	26°07′28″	80°59′00″	501666.20	2889465.50	Yes
LOOP1_H	NAVD 1988	Marsh structure	SFWMD	25°45′41″	80°54′28″	509247.95	2849262.84	Yes
LOOP1_T	NAVD 1988	Marsh structure	SFWMD	25°45′40″	80°54′28″	509247.97	2849232.08	Yes
LOOP2_H	NAVD 1988	Marsh structure	SFWMD	25°44′48″	80°57′14″	504624.55	2847630.07	Yes
LOOP2_T	NAVD 1988	Marsh structure	SFWMD	25°44′48″	80°57′15″	504596.69	2847630.06	Yes
Everglades National Park								
A13	NAVD 1988	Marsh	ENP	25°29′50″	80°42′45″	528893.78	2820037.51	Yes
C111_wetland_east_of_FIU_ LTER_TSPH5	NAVD 1988	Marsh	USGS	25°17′40″	80°31′12″	548320.95	2797638.29	Yes
CP	NAVD 1988	Marsh	ENP	25°13′39″	80°42′14″	529825.32	2790171.73	Yes
CR2	NAVD 1988	Marsh	ENP	25°29′55″	80°37′18″	538022.17	2820214.15	Yes
CR3	NAVD 1988	Marsh	ENP	25°29′48″	80°39′46″	533891.05	2819987.72	Yes
CT27R	NAVD 1988	Marsh	ENP	25°18′03″	80°29′19″	551478.18	2798357.45	Yes
CT50R	NAVD 1988	Marsh	ENP	25°18′46″	80°31′15″	548229.80	2799668.15	Yes
CV5NR	NAVD 1988	Marsh	ENP	25°18′08″	80°29′15″	551589.44	2798511.68	Yes
CY2	NAVD 1988	Marsh	ENP	25°19′39″	80°40′58″	531925.53	2801249.97	Yes

Appendix 1.   EDEN marsh stations, type of station, operating agency, location, and real-time status sorted by location (from Volin and others, 2008).—Continued

[NWIS, National Water Information System; UTM, Universal Transverse Mercator; NAVD 1988, North American Vertical Datum of 1988; NGVD 1929, National Geodetic Vertical Datum of 1929; BCNP, Big Cypress National Preserve; SFWMD, South Florida Water Management District; USGS, U.S. Geological Survey; ENP, Everglades National Park; , degrees; ′, minutes; ″, seconds]

Station name	Datum of data stored in NWIS	Type of station	Operating agency	Latitude	Longitude	UTM Easting	UTM Northing	Daily real-time data available?
			Everglades National Park—Continued					
CY3	NAVD 1988	Marsh	ENP	25°19′40″	80°45′02″	525104.23	2801266.29	Yes
DO1	NAVD 1988	Marsh	ENP	25°22′19″	80°41′27″	531103.44	2806169.62	Yes
DO2	NAVD 1988	Marsh	ENP	25°23′18″	80°44′39″	525734.39	2807973.10	Yes
E112	NAVD 1988	Marsh	ENP	25°25′26″	80°36′35″	539246.82	2811943.09	Yes
E146	NAVD 1988	Marsh	ENP	25°15′13″	80°39′59″	533595.29	2793071.95	Yes
EDEN_3	NAVD 1988	Marsh	USGS	25°30′44″	80°55′59″	506727.07	2821669.04	Yes
EPSW	NAVD 1988	Marsh	ENP	25°16′17″	80°30′29″	549532.76	2795089.58	Yes
EVER4	NGVD 1929	Marsh	USGS	25°20′37″	80°32′42″	545785.71	2803074.02	Yes
EVER6	NAVD 1988	Marsh	ENP	25°17′49″	80°30′41″	549186.82	2797918.26	Yes
EVER7	NAVD 1988	Marsh	ENP	25°18′31″	80°32′32″	546078.48	2799199.22	Yes
EVER8	NAVD 1988	Marsh	ENP	25°20′42″	80°28′42″	552493.75	2803252.29	Yes
L31W	NAVD 1988	Marsh	ENP	25°26′13″	80°35′23″	541253.62	2813394.85	Yes
MET1	NAVD 1988	Marsh	USGS	25°43′13″	80°35′18″	541295.94	2844771.35	Yes
NCL	NAVD 1988	Marsh	ENP	25°14′33″	80°44′40″	525737.25	2791824.34	Yes
NE1	NGVD 1929	Marsh	USGS	25°41′31″	80°38′04″	536678.99	2841620.09	Yes
NE2	NGVD 1929	Marsh	USGS	25°43′16″	80°33′14″	544750.93	2844874.86	Yes
NE4	NGVD 1929	Marsh	USGS	25°38′29″	80°39′10″	534854.15	2836016.61	Yes
NE5	NGVD 1929	Marsh	USGS	25°37′54″	80°39′35″	534159.83	2834938.17	Yes
NESRS3	NAVD 1988	Marsh	SFWMD	25°44′26″	80°30′16″	549702.86	2847045.87	No
NP201	NAVD 1988	Marsh	ENP	25°43′00″	80°43′10″	528144.43	2844336.98	Yes
NP202	NAVD 1988	Marsh	ENP	25°39′43″	80°42′31″	529244.56	2838279.40	Yes
NP203	NAVD 1988	Marsh	ENP	25°37′22″	80°44′19″	526242.23	2833935.83	Yes
NP205	NAVD 1988	Marsh	ENP	25°41′19″	80°50′52″	515273.99	2841209.02	Yes
NP206	NAVD 1988	Marsh	ENP	25°32′39″	80°40′19″	532956.81	2825245.45	Yes
NP44	NAVD 1988	Marsh	ENP	25°26′00″	80°43′13″	528126.95	2812961.02	Yes
NP46	NAVD 1988	Marsh	ENP	25°19′06″	80°47′45″	520549.03	2800212.76	Yes
NP62	NAVD 1988	Marsh	ENP	25°26′18″	80°46′58″	521841.46	2813502.99	Yes
NP67	NAVD 1988	Marsh	ENP	25°19′46″	80°39′01″	535195.83	2801473.43	Yes
NP72	NAVD 1988	Marsh	ENP	25°23′41″	80°42′11″	529868.22	2808689.13	Yes
NTS1	NAVD 1988	Marsh	ENP	25°26′12″	80°35′34″	540946.47	2813363.15	Yes
NTS10	NAVD 1988	Marsh	ENP	25°27′37″	80°36′18″	539709.76	2815974.08	Yes
NTS14	NAVD 1988	Marsh	ENP	25°24′59″	80°38′19″	536343.94	2811104.39	Yes
NTS18	NAVD 1988	Marsh	ENP	25°29′02″	80°33′59″	543582.91	2818600.78	Yes
OL	NAVD 1988	Marsh	ENP	25°15′49″	80°36′47″	538962.92	2794193.70	Yes
OT	NAVD 1988	Marsh	ENP	25°34′43″	80°57′52″	503570.92	2829019.52	Yes
P33	NAVD 1988	Marsh	ENP	25°36′50″	80°42′08″	529897.73	2832959.20	Yes
P34	NAVD 1988	Marsh	ENP	25°36′27″	80°56′27″	505940.80	2832219.45	Yes
P35	NAVD 1988	Marsh	ENP	25°27′35″	80°51′52″	513627.54	2815860.64	Yes
P36	NAVD 1988	Marsh	ENP	25°31′38″	80°47′44″	520541.55	2823344.19	Yes

Appendix 1. EDEN marsh stations, type of station, operating agency, location, and real-time status sorted by location (from Volin and others, 2008).—Continued

[NWIS, National Water Information System; UTM, Universal Transverse Mercator; NAVD 1988, North American Vertical Datum of 1988; NGVD 1929, National Geodetic Vertical Datum of 1929; BCNP, Big Cypress National Preserve; SFWMD, South Florida Water Management District; USGS, U.S. Geological Survey; ENP, Everglades National Park; , degrees; ′, minutes; ″, seconds]

Station name	Datum of data stored in NWIS	Type of station	Operating agency	Latitude	Longitude	UTM Easting	UTM Northing	Daily real-time data available?
	Everglades National Park—Continued							
P37	NAVD 1988	Marsh	ENP	25°17′03″	80°41′18″	531377.57	2796450.17	Yes
P38	NAVD 1988	Marsh	ENP	25°22′10″	80°50′00″	516767.66	2805867.27	Yes
R127	NAVD 1988	Marsh	ENP	25°21′11″	80°36′22″	539633.08	2804100.35	Yes
R3110	NAVD 1988	Marsh	ENP	25°26′46″	80°37′34″	537591.82	2814399.18	Yes
RG1	NAVD 1988	Marsh	ENP	25°34′53″	80°36′28″	539390.95	2829384.86	Yes
RG2	NAVD 1988	Marsh	ENP	25°32′33″	80°36′21″	539599.02	2825078.93	Yes
SP	NAVD 1988	Marsh	ENP	25°23′19″	80°47′50″	520397.44	2807994.71	Yes
Taylor_Slough_wetland_at_E146	NAVD 1988	Marsh	USGS	25°14′57″	80°39′58″	533624.49	2792579.87	Yes
TMC	NAVD 1988	Marsh	ENP	25°36′50″	80°52′20″	512829.22	2832931.80	Yes
TS2	NAVD 1988	Marsh	ENP	25°24′00″	80°36′24″	539561.88	2809298.62	Yes
TSH	NAVD 1988	Marsh	ENP	25°18′39″	80°37′50″	537186.36	2799417.86	Yes
S12A_T	NGVD 1929	Marsh structure	USGS	25°45′41″	80°49′16″	517938.81	2849271.77	Yes
S12B_T	NGVD 1929	Marsh structure	USGS	25°45′42″	80°46′10″	523119.86	2849310.58	Yes
S12C_T	NGVD 1929	Marsh structure	USGS	25°45′42″	80°43′37″	527381.73	2849318.72	Yes
S12D_T	NGVD 1929	Marsh structure	USGS	25°45′42″	80°40′55″	531894.31	2849328.84	Yes
S332B_T	NAVD 1988	Marsh structure	SFWMD	25°32′58″	80°33′38″	544145.25	2825862.22	Yes
S332_T	NAVD 1988	Marsh structure	SFWMD	25°25′19″	80°35′26″	541174.92	2811733.54	Yes
	Water Conservation Area 1							
[1]NORTH_CA1	NGVD 1929	Marsh	USGS	26°35′38″	80°21′13″	564361.19	2941618.52	Yes
SITE_7	NGVD 1929	Marsh	USGS	26°31′11″	80°20′49″	565066.87	2933407.44	Yes
SITE_8C	NGVD 1929	Marsh	USGS	26°30′01″	80°13′21″	577479.30	2931322.94	Yes
SITE_8T	NGVD 1929	Marsh	USGS	26°29′59″	80°14′05″	576261.65	2931254.09	Yes
SITE_9	NGVD 1929	Marsh	USGS	26°27′51″	80°17′49″	570082.42	2927280.64	Yes
[1]SOUTH_CA1	NGVD 1929	Marsh	USGS	26°25′29″	80°20′26″	565757.42	2922888.94	Yes
WCA1ME	NAVD 1988	Marsh	SFWMD	26°30′39″	80°18′36″	568753.21	2932442.20	Yes
	Water Conservation Area 2A							
2A300	NAVD 1988	Marsh	SFWMD	26°14′47″	80°24′29″	559116.94	2903105.37	No
EDEN_11	NAVD 1988	Marsh	USGS	26°22′58″	80°27′35″	553893.80	2918188.10	Yes
SITE_17	NGVD 1929	Marsh	USGS	26°17′12″	80°24′39″	558819.22	2907564.92	Yes
SITE_19	NGVD 1929	Marsh	USGS	26°16′56″	80°18′22″	569277.05	2907124.53	Yes
WCA2E1	NAVD 1988	Marsh	SFWMD	26°21′07″	80°21′10″	564579.11	2914822.32	No
WCA2E4	NAVD 1988	Marsh	SFWMD	26°18′35″	80°21′23″	564242.08	2910144.28	No
WCA2F1	NAVD 1988	Marsh	SFWMD	26°21′36″	80°22′11″	562884.01	2915706.13	No
WCA2F4	NAVD 1988	Marsh	SFWMD	26°19′02″	80°23′05″	561409.97	2910961.15	No
WCA2RT	NAVD 1988	Marsh	SFWMD	26°19′48″	80°30′35″	548928.32	2912322.94	No
WCA2U1	NAVD 1988	Marsh	SFWMD	26°14′29″	80°21′21″	564335.21	2902576.49	No
WCA2U3	NAVD 1988	Marsh	SFWMD	26°17′17″	80°24′39″	558818.52	2907718.74	No
S10A_T	NGVD 1929	Marsh structure	USGS	26°21′33″	80°18′46″	568566.11	2915642.85	Yes

Appendix 1.   EDEN marsh stations, type of station, operating agency, location, and real-time status sorted by location (from Volin and others, 2008).—Continued

[NWIS, National Water Information System; UTM, Universal Transverse Mercator; NAVD 1988, North American Vertical Datum of 1988; NGVD 1929, National Geodetic Vertical Datum of 1929; BCNP, Big Cypress National Preserve; SFWMD, South Florida Water Management District; USGS, U.S. Geological Survey; ENP, Everglades National Park; ˚, degrees; ′, minutes; ″, seconds]

Station name	Datum of data stored in NWIS	Type of station	Operating agency	Latitude	Longitude	UTM Easting	UTM Northing	Daily real-time data available?
Water Conservation Area 2A—Continued								
S10C_T	NGVD 1929	Marsh structure	USGS	26°22′16″	80°21′09″	564596.17	2916945.24	Yes
S10D_T	NGVD 1929	Marsh structure	USGS	26°23′18″	80°22′55″	561649.51	2918838.25	Yes
S11A_H	NGVD 1929	Marsh structure	USGS	26°10′37″	80°26′54″	555127.07	2895396.64	Yes
S11B_H	NGVD 1929	Marsh structure	USGS	26°12′09″	80°27′14″	554559.99	2898224.56	Yes
S11C_H	NGVD 1929	Marsh structure	USGS	26°13′47″	80°27′35″	553964.64	2901236.98	Yes
S144_H	NAVD 1988	Marsh structure	SFWMD	26°13′06″	80°23′52″	560157.83	2900002.92	No
S145_H	NAVD 1988	Marsh structure	SFWMD	26°13′19″	80°21′57″	563346.98	2900418.07	No
S146_H	NAVD 1988	Marsh structure	SFWMD	26°13′32″	80°20′01″	566563.70	2900834.14	No
Water Conservation Area 2B								
EDEN_13	NAVD 1988	Marsh	USGS	26°10′35″	80°22′17″	562816.46	2895370.05	Yes
SITE_99	NGVD 1929	Marsh	USGS	26°08′14″	80°22′01″	563281.73	2891034.49	Yes
S141_H	NAVD 1988	Marsh structure	SFWMD	26°09′02″	80°26′32″	555750.30	2892476.69	No
S144_T	NAVD 1988	Marsh structure	SFWMD	26°13′05″	80°23′52″	560157.97	2899972.15	No
S145_T	NAVD 1988	Marsh structure	SFWMD	26°13′18″	80°21′57″	563347.13	2900387.30	No
S146_T	NAVD 1988	Marsh structure	SFWMD	26°13′31″	80°20′00″	566591.60	2900803.52	No
Water Conservation Area 3A								
3A10	NAVD 1988	Marsh	SFWMD	26°16′46″	80°44′23″	525986.11	2906657.28	No
3A11	NAVD 1988	Marsh	SFWMD	26°13′06″	80°44′37″	525611.24	2899888.56	No
3A12	NAVD 1988	Marsh	SFWMD	26°10′09″	80°40′32″	532423.10	2894458.68	No
3A5	NAVD 1988	Marsh	USGS	26°03′24″	80°42′19″	529481.03	2881992.65	Yes
3A9	NAVD 1988	Marsh	SFWMD	26°07′23″	80°38′51″	535240.68	2889359.31	No
3AN1W1	NAVD 1988	Marsh	SFWMD	26°11′17″	80°44′24″	525978.68	2896536.09	Yes
3ANE	NAVD 1988	Marsh	SFWMD	26°16′44″	80°36′17″	539464.80	2906629.89	Yes
3ANW	NAVD 1988	Marsh	SFWMD	26°16′00″	80°46′49″	521939.44	2905234.65	Yes
3AS	NAVD 1988	Marsh	SFWMD	26°05′01″	80°41′03″	531585.55	2884981.57	Yes
3AS3W1	NAVD 1988	Marsh	SFWMD	25°51′27″	80°46′15″	522962.10	2859923.05	Yes
3ASW	NAVD 1988	Marsh	SFWMD	25°59′24″	80°50′09″	516430.82	2874586.72	Yes
EDEN_12	NAVD 1988	Marsh	USGS	26°00′42″	80°35′17″	541222.59	2877040.84	Yes
EDEN_14	NAVD 1988	Marsh	USGS	26°04′10″	80°45′27″	524254.59	2883396.97	Yes
EDEN_4	NAVD 1988	Marsh	USGS	26°05′36″	80°30′25″	549305.17	2886113.29	Yes
EDEN_5	NAVD 1988	Marsh	USGS	26°07′25″	80°45′10″	524715.52	2889396.58	Yes
EDEN_8	NAVD 1988	Marsh	USGS	25°52′00″	80°40′50″	532005.36	2860957.08	Yes
EDEN_9	NAVD 1988	Marsh	USGS	26°13′19″	80°35′32″	540732.67	2900327.21	Yes
SITE_62	NGVD 1929	Marsh	USGS	26°10′29″	80°45′04″	524871.31	2895057.28	Yes
SITE_63	NGVD 1929	Marsh	USGS	26°11′20″	80°31′51″	546878.08	2896687.07	Yes
SITE_64	NGVD 1929	Marsh	USGS	25°58′32″	80°40′09″	533115.99	2873018.65	Yes
SITE_65	NGVD 1929	Marsh	USGS	25°48′53″	80°43′11″	528093.47	2855195.68	Yes

Appendix 1. EDEN marsh stations, type of station, operating agency, location, and real-time status sorted by location (from Volin and others, 2008).—Continued

[NWIS, National Water Information System; UTM, Universal Transverse Mercator; NAVD 1988, North American Vertical Datum of 1988; NGVD 1929, National Geodetic Vertical Datum of 1929; BCNP, Big Cypress National Preserve; SFWMD, South Florida Water Management District; USGS, U.S. Geological Survey; ENP, Everglades National Park; °, degrees; ′, minutes; ″, seconds]

Station name	Datum of data stored in NWIS	Type of station	Operating agency	Latitude	Longitude	UTM Easting	UTM Northing	Daily real-time data available?
Water Conservation Area 3A—Continued								
W11	NAVD 1988	Marsh	USGS	25°56′34″	80°45′00″	525031.57	2869370.75	Yes
W14	NAVD 1988	Marsh	USGS	25°56′14″	80°40′06″	533210.16	2868773.67	Yes
W15	NAVD 1988	Marsh	USGS	26°00′51″	80°40′40″	532243.48	2877292.48	Yes
W18	NAVD 1988	Marsh	USGS	26°00′07″	80°46′44″	522127.95	2875917.89	Yes
W2	NAVD 1988	Marsh	USGS	25°47′59″	80°48′32″	519158.29	2853518.55	Yes
W5	NAVD 1988	Marsh	USGS	25°47′21″	80°41′43″	530550.21	2852371.06	Yes
S11A_T	NGVD 1929	Marsh structure	USGS	26°10′37″	80°26′57″	555043.79	2895396.28	Yes
S11B_T	NGVD 1929	Marsh structure	USGS	26°12′09″	80°27′18″	554448.98	2898224.09	Yes
S11C_T	NGVD 1929	Marsh structure	USGS	26°13′46″	80°27′39″	553853.78	2901205.76	Yes
S142_T	NAVD 1988	Marsh structure	SFWMD	26°09′36″	80°26′47″	555329.37	2893520.88	No
[1]S150_T (SFWMD)	NAVD 1988	Marsh structure	SFWMD	26°20′05″	80°32′22″	545960.23	2912835.01	Yes
[1]S150_T (USGS)	NAVD 1988	Marsh structure	USGS	26°20′05″	80°32′22″	545960.23	2912835.01	No
S343A_H	NAVD 1988	Marsh structure	SFWMD	25°47′21″	80°51′19″	514509.23	2852343.69	Yes
S343B_H	NAVD 1988	Marsh structure	SFWMD	25°46′42″	80°50′38″	515652.45	2851145.31	Yes
S344_H	NAVD 1988	Marsh structure	SFWMD	25°55′08″	80°50′11″	516385.06	2866711.57	Yes
Water Conservation Area 3B								
3BS1W1	NAVD 1988	Marsh	SFWMD	25°46′50″	80°30′40″	549017.78	2851473.08	Yes
3BSE	NAVD 1988	Marsh	SFWMD	25°47′17″	80°29′58″	550184.38	2852308.04	No
EDEN_10	NAVD 1988	Marsh	USGS	25°47′07″	80°37′02″	538377.06	2851960.83	Yes
EDEN_7	NAVD 1988	Marsh	USGS	25°57′08″	80°29′55″	550198.51	2870488.89	Yes
SITE_69	NGVD 1929	Marsh	USGS	25°54′24″	80°35′20″	541175.72	2865412.37	Yes
SITE_71	NGVD 1929	Marsh	USGS	25°53′05″	80°33′24″	544411.25	2862992.67	Yes
SITE_76	NGVD 1929	Marsh	USGS	26°00′28″	80°28′57″	551787.22	2876647.73	Yes
SRS1	NGVD 1929	Marsh	USGS	25°47′55″	80°34′42″	542271.35	2853449.30	Yes
TI8	NAVD 1988	Marsh	USGS	25°49′57″	80°32′28″	545989.77	2857214.74	Yes
TI9	NAVD 1988	Marsh	USGS	25°50′14″	80°35′58″	540141.95	2857718.58	Yes
S9A_T	NAVD 1988	Marsh structure	SFWMD	26°03′41″	80°26′38″	555625.88	2882600.90	Yes
Florida Bay (Tidal River)								
Joe_Bay_2E	NAVD 1988	River	USGS	25°13′55″	80°31′28″	547898.04	2790715.76	Yes
McCormick_Creek_at_mouth	NAVD 1988	River	USGS	25°10′04″	80°43′54″	527040.62	2783552.68	Yes
Mud_Creek_at_mouth	NAVD 1988	River	USGS	25°12′12″	80°35′00″	541976.49	2787527.86	Yes
Stillwater_Creek	NAVD 1988	River	USGS	25°13′42″	80°29′11″	551732.6	2790329.99	Yes
Upstream_Taylor_River	NAVD 1988	River	USGS	25°12′42″	80°38′52″	535481.65	2788432.09	Yes
Taylor_River_at_mouth	NAVD 1988	River	USGS	25°11′28″	80°38′20″	536383.20	2786158.28	Yes
Trout_Creek_at_mouth	NAVD 1988	River	USGS	25°12′54″	80°32′00″	547009.25	2788836.29	Yes
West_Highway_Creek	NAVD 1988	River	USGS	25°14′34″	80°26′49″	555699.07	2791945.27	Yes

Appendix 1. EDEN marsh stations, type of station, operating agency, location, and real-time status sorted by location (from Volin and others, 2008).—Continued

[NWIS, National Water Information System; UTM, Universal Transverse Mercator; NAVD 1988, North American Vertical Datum of 1988; NGVD 1929, National Geodetic Vertical Datum of 1929; BCNP, Big Cypress National Preserve; SFWMD, South Florida Water Management District; USGS, U.S. Geological Survey; ENP, Everglades National Park; , degrees; ′, minutes; ″, seconds]

Station name	Datum of data stored in NWIS	Type of station	Operating agency	Latitude	Longitude	UTM Easting	UTM Northing	Daily real-time data available?
Gulf of Mexico (Tidal Rivers)								
Bottle_Creek_at_Rookery_ Branch	NAVD 1988	River	USGS	25°28′06″	80°51′15″	514652.96	2816827.80	Yes
Broad_River_near_the_Cutoff	NAVD 1988	River	USGS	25°30′06″	81°04′36″	492287.91	2820513.20	Yes
Upstream_Broad_River	NAVD 1988	River	USGS	25°30′04.7″	80°55′56″	506811.43	2820460.20	Yes
Chatham_River_near_the_ Watson_Place	NAVD 1988	River	USGS	25°42′34″	81°14′58″	474967.37	2843542.60	Yes
Harney_River	NAVD 1988	River	USGS	25°25′52.4″	81°05′08.3″	491388.61	2812700.50	Yes
Lopez_River_Near_Lopez_ Campsite	NAVD 1988	River	USGS	25°47′30″	81°17′58″	469971.82	2852658.10	Yes
Lostmans_River_below_ Second_Bay	NAVD 1988	River	USGS	25°33′21″	81°09′52″	483473.78	2826506.90	Yes
Upstream_Lostmans_River	NAVD 1988	River	USGS	25°33′57″	80°59′41″	500530.11	2827604.10	Yes
New_River_at_Sunday_Bay	NAVD 1988	River	USGS	25°47′52″	81°15′19″	474401.14	2853325.50	Yes
North_River_Upstream_of_ Cutoff	NAVD 1988	River	USGS	25°20′19″	80°54′47″	508742.28	2802458.40	Yes
Upstream_North_River	NAVD 1988	River	USGS	25°21′29″	80°54′00″	510026.00	2804598.00	Yes
Shark_River_Below_Gunboat_ Island	NAVD 1988	River	USGS	25°22′31″	81°02′12″	496303.90	2806516.30	Yes
Turner_River_nr_Chokoloskee_ Island	NAVD 1988	River	USGS	25°49′44″	81°20′29″	465777.31	2856790.20	Yes

[1] Prior to October 1, 2004, data stored in NGVD 1929.

Appendix 2. EDEN canal station, type of station, operating agency, location, and real-time status sorted by location (from Volin and others, 2008).

[NWIS, National Water Information System; UTM, Universal Transverse Mercator; NAVD 1988, North American Vertical Datum of 1988; NGVD 1929, National Geodetic Vertical Datum of 1929; USGS, U.S. Geological Survey; SFWMD, South Florida Water Management District; ˚, degrees; ´, minutes; ˝, seconds]

Station name	Datum of data stored in NWIS	Type of station	Operating agency	Latitude	Longitude	UTM Easting	UTM Northing	Daily real-time data available?
				C111 Canal				
S18C_T	NGVD 1929	Canal structure	USGS	25°19´15˝	80°31´30˝	547807.24	2800558.69	Yes
L28	NAVD 1988	Canal						
L28S1	NAVD 1988	Canal	SFWMD	26°05´38˝	80°50´34˝	515721.92	2886090.99	Yes
L28S2	NAVD 1988	Canal	SFWMD	26°05´38˝	80°50´05˝	516527.46	2886091.99	Yes
S140_H	NAVD 1988	Canal structure	SFWMD	26°10´18˝	80°49´40˝	517210.49	2894706.47	Yes
S343A_T	NAVD 1988	Canal structure	SFWMD	25°47´20˝	80°51´20˝	514481.41	2852312.90	Yes
S343B_T	NAVD 1988	Canal structure	SFWMD	25°46´41˝	80°50´39˝	515624.64	2851114.51	Yes
				L28 Interceptor Canal				
S190_T	NAVD 1988	Canal structure	SFWMD	26°16´60˝	80°58´04˝	503216.95	2907062.23	Yes
				L30 Canal				
S335_H	NAVD 1988	Canal structure	SFWMD	25°46´34˝	80°28´59˝	551832.70	2850991.63	Yes
S335_T	NAVD 1988	Canal structure	SFWMD	25°46´32˝	80°28´59˝	551832.95	2850930.10	Yes
S337_T	NAVD 1988	Canal structure	SFWMD	25°56´30˝	80°26´28˝	555960.44	2869343.21	Yes
				L31N Canal				
L31N_1	NGVD 1929	Canal	USGS	25°44´54˝	80°29´52˝	550368.24	2847909.73	Yes
L31N_3	NGVD 1929	Canal	USGS	25°44´48˝	80°29´51˝	550396.80	2847725.26	Yes
L31N_4	NGVD 1929	Canal	USGS	25°42´07˝	80°29´45˝	550582.88	2842773.27	Yes
L31N_5	NGVD 1929	Canal	USGS	25°41´10˝	80°29´49˝	550478.07	2841019.43	Yes
L31N_7	NGVD 1929	Canal	USGS	25°39´48˝	80°29´53˝	550376.15	2838496.57	Yes
L31NN	NAVD 1988	Canal	SFWMD	25°44´47˝	80°29´51˝	550396.92	2847694.50	Yes
L31NS	NAVD 1988	Canal	SFWMD	25°42´08˝	80°29´45˝	550582.76	2842804.03	Yes
G211_H	NAVD 1988	Canal structure	SFWMD	25°39´36˝	80°29´52˝	550405.43	2838127.53	Yes
G211_T	NAVD 1988	Canal structure	SFWMD	25°39´33˝	80°29´52˝	550405.78	2838035.25	Yes
				L31W Canal				
S175_H	NAVD 1988	Canal structure	SFWMD	25°25´05˝	80°34´26˝	542852.37	2811308.15	Yes
S175_T	NAVD 1988	Canal structure	SFWMD	25°25´03˝	80°34´26˝	542852.56	2811246.63	Yes
S332D_T	NAVD 1988	Canal structure	SFWMD	25°28´59˝	80°33´51˝	543806.57	2818509.23	Yes
				L38E Canal				
S141_T	NAVD 1988	Canal structure	SFWMD	26°09´03˝	80°26´33˝	555722.40	2892507.33	No
S142_H	NAVD 1988	Canal structure	SFWMD	26°09´37˝	80°26´41˝	555495.81	2893552.35	No
S143_T	NAVD 1988	Canal structure	SFWMD	26°10´34˝	80°26´54˝	555127.46	2895304.34	No
S34_H	NAVD 1988	Canal structure	SFWMD	26°09´02˝	80°26´33˝	555722.53	2892476.57	Yes
S7_T	NAVD 1988	Canal structure	SFWMD	26°20´07˝	80°32´12˝	546237.21	2912897.53	Yes
				L39 Canal				
S10A_H	NGVD 1929	Canal structure	USGS	26°21´36˝	80°18´45˝	568593.34	2915735.29	Yes
S10C_H	NGVD 1929	Canal structure	USGS	26°22´18˝	80°21´09˝	564595.86	2917006.77	Yes
S10D_H	NGVD 1929	Canal structure	USGS	26°23´19˝	80°22´54˝	561677.07	2918869.15	Yes
S39_H	NAVD 1988	Canal structure	SFWMD	26°21´21˝	80°17´53˝	570037.05	2915281.57	Yes

Appendix 2. EDEN canal station, type of station, operating agency, location, and real-time status sorted by location (from Volin and others, 2008).—Continued

[NWIS, National Water Information System; UTM, Universal Transverse Mercator; NAVD 1988, North American Vertical Datum of 1988; NGVD 1929, National Geodetic Vertical Datum of 1929; USGS, U.S. Geological Survey; SFWMD, South Florida Water Management District; , degrees; ´, minutes; ˝, seconds]

Station name	Datum of data stored in NWIS	Type of station	Operating agency	Latitude	Longitude	UTM Easting	UTM Northing	Daily real-time data available?
				L40 Canal				
G300_T	NAVD 1988	Canal structure	SFWMD	26°40´37˝	80°21´48˝	563347.29	2950812.7	Yes
				L6 Canal				
G339_H	NAVD 1988	Canal structure	SFWMD	26°27´48˝	80°27´09˝	554576.30	2927112.93	Yes
G339_T	NAVD 1988	Canal structure	SFWMD	26°27´48˝	80°27´10˝	554548.61	2927112.81	Yes
				L7 Canal				
G301_T	NAVD 1988	Canal structure	SFWMD	26°40´31˝	80°22´49˝	561662.20	2950619.81	Yes
				Miami Canal				
S151_H	NAVD 1988	Canal structure	SFWMD	26°00´42˝	80°30´36˝	549033.58	2877067.80	Yes
S151_T	NAVD 1988	Canal structure	SFWMD	26°00´40˝	80°30´35˝	549061.61	2877006.38	Yes
S31_H	NAVD 1988	Canal structure	SFWMD	25°56´33˝	80°26´26˝	556015.68	2869435.74	Yes
S339_H	NAVD 1988	Canal structure	SFWMD	26°13´04˝	80°41´27˝	530883.50	2899838.53	Yes
S339_T	NAVD 1988	Canal structure	SFWMD	26°13´01˝	80°41´25˝	530939.22	2899746.37	Yes
S340_H	NAVD 1988	Canal structure	SFWMD	26°07´09˝	80°36´48˝	538657.75	2888938.33	Yes
S340_T	NAVD 1988	Canal structure	SFWMD	26°07´06˝	80°36´45˝	538741.34	2888846.29	Yes
S8_T	NGVD 1929	Canal structure	USGS	26°19´52˝	80°46´27˝	522537.17	2912372.84	Yes
				North Feeder Canal				
S190_H	NAVD 1988	Canal structure	SFWMD	26°17´03˝	80°58´05˝	503189.19	2907154.51	Yes
				Pennsuco Wetlands				
NWWF	NGVD 1929	Canal	USGS	25°53´28˝	80°25´13˝	558071.25	2863753.46	Yes
S380_H	NAVD 1988	Canal structure	SFWMD	25°45´41˝	80°26´54˝	555321.10	2849375.36	Yes
				Tamiami Canal				
G119_H	NAVD 1988	Canal structure	SFWMD	25°45´40˝	80°28´39˝	552396.34	2849332.68	No
G119_T	NAVD 1988	Canal structure	SFWMD	25°45´40˝	80°28´37˝	552452.05	2849332.9	No
S12A_H	NGVD 1929	Canal structure	USGS	25°45´44˝	80°49´16˝	517938.69	2849364.06	Yes
S12B_H	NGVD 1929	Canal structure	USGS	25°45´44˝	80°46´10˝	523119.75	2849372.10	Yes
S12C_H	NGVD 1929	Canal structure	USGS	25°45´44˝	80°43´37˝	527381.60	2849380.24	Yes
S12D_H	NGVD 1929	Canal structure	USGS	25°45´44˝	80°40´54˝	531922.02	2849390.43	Yes
S333_H	NAVD 1988	Canal structure	SFWMD	25°45´43˝	80°40´27˝	532674.19	2849361.50	Yes
S333_T	NAVD 1988	Canal structure	SFWMD	25°45´42˝	80°40´23˝	532785.69	2849331.02	Yes
S334_H	NAVD 1988	Canal structure	SFWMD	25°45´41˝	80°30´10˝	549861.33	2849353.64	Yes
S334_T	NAVD 1988	Canal structure	SFWMD	25°45´41˝	80°30´05˝	550000.61	2849354.16	Yes
S336_H	NAVD 1988	Canal structure	SFWMD	25°45´40˝	80°29´50˝	550418.56	2849324.99	Yes
S336_T	NAVD 1988	Canal structure	SFWMD	25°45´40˝	80°29´48˝	550474.28	2849325.20	Yes
S344_T	NAVD 1988	Canal structure	SFWMD	25°55´08˝	80°50´12˝	516357.24	2866711.54	Yes
				Water Conservation Area 3A				
S140_T	NAVD 1988	Canal structure	SFWMD	26°10´18˝	80°49´38˝	517266.00	2894706.55	Yes

Appendix 3.   EDEN water-level estimation equations and performance statistics sorted by station name.

[n, number of data points; R^2, coefficient of determination; RMSE, root mean square error; WCA, Water Conservation Area; ENP, Everglades National Park; BCNP, Big Cypress National Preserve; FB, Florida Bay]

Station name[a]	Predictor number[a]	Predictor station name[a]	Slope, m	y-intercept, b	Pearson correlation coefficient	Minimum observed[a]	Maximum observed[a]	n	R^2	Mean error	RMSE	Standard error	Average measured, in feet[a]	Nash-Sutcliffe	Percent model error	Percent model bias	Area of site[a]	Area of predictor
2A300	P1	S146_H	0.92	1.80	0.99	8.80	13.10	2248	0.983	-0.00	0.12	0.12	10.647	0.98	2.7	-0.0	WCA 2A	WCA 2A
2A300	P2	S145_H	0.93	1.31	0.99	—	—	2642	0.972	-0.01	0.16	0.16	—	0.97	3.7	-0.1	WCA 2A	WCA 2A
2A300	P3	S144_H	0.92	1.34	0.99	—	—	2735	0.969	0.00	0.17	0.16	—	0.97	3.9	0.0	WCA 2A	WCA 2A
2A300	P4	—	—	—	—	—	—	—	—	—	—	—	—	—	—	—	WCA 2A	—
3A10	P1	3ANW	0.89	0.97	0.95	8.55	11.30	1632	0.888	-0.02	0.21	0.20	9.764	0.89	7.5	-0.2	WCA 3A	WCA 3A
3A10	P2	3AN1W1	0.91	1.20	0.91	—	—	1172	0.859	-0.01	0.22	0.20	—	0.86	8.1	-0.1	WCA 3A	WCA 3A
3A10	P3	SITE_62	0.91	-0.30	0.91	—	—	2063	0.853	-0.01	0.24	0.21	—	0.85	8.5	-0.1	WCA 3A	WCA 3A
3A10	P4	—	—	—	—	—	—	—	—	—	—	—	—	—	—	—	WCA 3A	—
3A11	P1	3AN1W1	0.95	1.25	0.98	9.07	11.88	1683	0.966	0.00	0.12	0.12	10.308	0.97	4.2	0.0	WCA 3A	WCA 3A
3A11	P2	SITE_62	0.89	0.49	0.97	—	—	2378	0.942	0.00	0.15	0.14	—	0.94	5.3	0.0	WCA 3A	WCA 3A
3A11	P3	3ANW	0.84	1.99	0.95	—	—	1642	0.872	-0.04	0.23	0.22	—	0.87	8.2	-0.4	WCA 3A	WCA 3A
3A11	P4	—	—	—	—	—	—	—	—	—	—	—	—	—	—	—	WCA 3A	—
3A12	P1	3A9	0.96	-0.10	0.99	6.77	10.57	2902	0.976	0.00	0.11	0.11	8.803	0.98	2.8	0.0	WCA 3A	WCA 3A
3A12	P2	SITE_62	0.98	-2.06	0.98	—	—	2961	0.960	0.00	0.14	0.13	—	0.96	3.6	0.0	WCA 3A	WCA 3A
3A12	P3	3AN1W1	1.08	-1.52	0.98	—	—	1784	0.952	-0.00	0.16	0.15	—	0.95	4.2	-0.0	WCA 3A	WCA 3A
3A12	P4	—	—	—	—	—	—	—	—	—	—	—	—	—	—	—	WCA 3A	—
3A-5	P1	3AS	0.95	0.40	0.99	8.15	10.19	728	0.982	0.00	0.06	0.06	8.755	0.98	3.0	0.0	WCA 3A	WCA 3A
3A-5	P2	EDEN_14	0.93	0.66	0.98	—	—	668	0.955	-0.00	0.09	0.09	—	0.96	4.4	-0.0	WCA 3A	WCA 3A
3A-5	P3	W18	0.91	1.07	0.97	—	—	663	0.946	0.00	0.11	0.10	—	0.95	5.2	0.0	WCA 3A	WCA 3A
3A-5	P4	—	—	—	—	—	—	—	—	—	—	—	—	—	—	—	WCA 3A	—
3A9	P1	3A12	1.01	0.33	0.99	6.96	11.05	2902	0.976	0.00	0.11	0.11	9.250	0.98	2.7	0.0	WCA 3A	WCA 3A
3A9	P2	3AS	1.02	0.09	0.98	—	—	2682	0.959	-0.00	0.15	0.15	—	0.96	3.8	0.0	WCA 3A	WCA 3A
3A9	P3	3AN1W1	1.12	-1.41	0.97	—	—	1839	0.945	-0.00	0.19	0.18	—	0.95	4.5	-0.0	WCA 3A	WCA 3A
3A9	P4	—	—	—	—	—	—	—	—	—	—	—	—	—	—	—	WCA 3A	—
3AN1W1	P1	SITE_62	0.89	-0.25	0.99	8.02	11.20	1882	0.971	0.00	0.12	0.12	9.586	0.97	3.7	0.0	WCA 3A	WCA 3A
3AN1W1	P2	3A12	0.88	1.80	0.98	—	—	1784	0.952	0.00	0.14	0.14	—	0.95	4.5	0.0	WCA 3A	WCA 3A
3AN1W1	P3	EDEN_5	0.99	0.60	0.96	—	—	674	0.932	0.00	0.13	0.12	—	0.94	3.9	0.0	WCA 3A	WCA 3A
3AN1W1	P4	—	—	—	—	—	—	—	—	—	—	—	—	—	—	—	WCA 3A	—
3ANE	P1	EDEN_9	0.98	0.55	0.96	7.91	11.15	613	0.923	0.00	0.17	0.16	9.336	0.94	5.2	0.0	WCA 3A	WCA 3A
3ANE	P2	3A9	1.00	0.04	0.95	—	—	2599	0.911	0.00	0.22	0.21	—	0.91	6.9	0.0	WCA 3A	WCA 3A
3ANE	P3	3AN1W1	1.13	-1.48	0.95	—	—	1855	0.903	0.00	0.25	0.24	—	0.90	7.9	0.0	WCA 3A	WCA 3A
3ANE	P4	—	—	—	—	—	—	—	—	—	—	—	—	—	—	—	WCA 3A	—
3ANW	P1	3A10	1.01	0.04	0.95	8.34	11.54	1632	0.888	0.02	0.22	0.21	10.064	0.89	6.9	0.2	WCA 3A	WCA 3A
3ANW	P2	3AN1W1	0.90	1.47	0.94	—	—	1313	0.849	0.05	0.25	0.23	—	0.85	7.8	0.5	WCA 3A	WCA 3A
3ANW	P3	SITE_62	0.96	-0.67	0.93	—	—	2197	0.821	0.04	0.29	0.26	—	0.82	9.1	0.4	WCA 3A	WCA 3A
3ANW	P4	—	—	—	—	—	—	—	—	—	—	—	—	—	—	—	WCA 3A	—

Appendix 3. EDEN water-level estimation equations and performance statistics sorted by station name.—Continued

[n, number of data points; R², coefficient of determination; RMSE, root mean square error; WCA, Water Conservation Area; ENP, Everglades National Park; BCNP, Big Cypress National Preserve; FB, Florida Bay]

[a]Station name	[a]Predictor number	Predictor station name	Slope, m	y-intercept, b	Pearson correlation coefficient	[a]Minimum observed	[a]Maximum observed	n	R²	Mean error	RMSE	Standard error	[a]Average measured, in feet	Nash-Sutcliffe	Percent model error	Percent model bias	Area of site	Area of predictor
3AS	P1	3A-5	1.03	−0.25	0.99	6.70	10.75	728	0.982	0.00	0.06	0.06	8.970	0.98	1.6	0.0	WCA 3A	WCA 3A
3AS	P2	3A9	0.94	0.29	0.98	—	—	2682	0.959	−0.00	0.15	0.15	—	0.96	3.7	−0.0	WCA 3A	WCA 3A
3AS	P3	EDEN_14	0.96	0.38	0.97	—	—	678	0.934	0.00	0.11	0.11	—	0.94	2.8	0.0	WCA 3A	WCA 3A
3AS	P4	—	—	—	—	—	—	—	—	—	—	—	—	—	—	—	WCA 3A	—
3AS3W1	P1	SITE_65	0.96	−0.97	0.99	6.56	9.75	2785	0.974	0.00	0.11	0.11	8.166	0.97	3.6	0.0	WCA 3A	WCA 3A
3AS3W1	P2	SITE_64	0.86	−0.52	0.98	—	—	2765	0.963	−0.00	0.14	0.13	—	0.96	4.3	−0.0	WCA 3A	WCA 3A
3AS3W1	P3	W5	0.92	0.82	0.97	—	—	1582	0.950	0.00	0.15	0.15	—	0.95	4.9	0.0	WCA 3A	WCA 3A
3AS3W1	P4	—	—	—	—	—	—	—	—	—	—	—	—	—	—	—	WCA 3A	—
3ASW	P1	S344_H	0.95	0.52	0.98	6.87	10.35	2677	0.964	0.00	0.14	0.14	8.667	0.96	4.1	0.0	WCA 3A	WCA 3A
3ASW	P2	S344_T	1.09	0.10	0.96	—	—	2638	0.924	−0.00	0.21	0.20	—	0.92	6.1	−0.0	WCA 3A	BCNP
3ASW	P3	W11	1.04	−0.08	0.97	—	—	1838	0.935	0.00	0.20	0.20	—	0.94	5.8	0.0	WCA 3A	WCA 3A
3ASW	P4	—	—	—	—	—	—	—	—	—	—	—	—	—	—	—	WCA 3A	—
3BS1W1	P1	SRS1	1.44	−5.64	0.98	2.72	6.92	2799	0.951	−0.00	0.19	0.19	5.138	0.95	4.5	−0.0	WCA 3B	WCA 3B
3BS1W1	P2	TI-8	1.73	−4.62	0.97	—	—	858	0.935	−0.00	0.20	0.19	—	0.95	4.7	−0.0	WCA 3B	WCA 3B
3BS1W1	P3	EDEN_10	2.05	−7.06	0.96	—	—	718	0.930	−0.00	0.21	0.20	—	0.95	4.9	−0.0	WCA 3B	WCA 3B
3BS1W1	P4	—	—	—	—	—	—	—	—	—	—	—	—	—	—	—	WCA 3B	—
3B-SE	P1	3BS1W1	1.08	−0.41	1.00	2.50	7.00	2234	0.998	0.00	0.04	0.04	5.205	1.00	1.0	0.0	WCA 3B	WCA 3B
3B-SE	P2	EDEN_10	2.20	−7.95	0.98	—	—	418	0.949	−0.01	0.16	0.16	—	0.95	3.6	−0.2	WCA 3B	WCA 3B
3B-SE	P3	TI-8	1.88	−5.43	0.97	—	—	554	0.936	0.03	0.19	0.19	—	0.94	4.3	0.5	WCA 3B	WCA 3B
3B-SE	P4	—	—	—	—	—	—	—	—	—	—	—	—	—	—	—	WCA 3B	—
A13	P1	CR3	0.85	−0.07	0.97	−0.72	4.72	3155	0.935	0.00	0.24	0.24	2.901	0.94	4.5	0.0	ENP	ENP
A13	P2	NP206	0.91	−0.73	0.96	—	—	3155	0.928	0.00	0.26	0.25	—	0.93	4.7	0.0	ENP	ENP
A13	P3	NP62	1.16	1.59	0.94	—	—	3139	0.889	0.00	0.32	0.30	—	0.89	5.9	0.0	ENP	ENP
A13	P4	—	—	—	—	—	—	—	—	—	—	—	—	—	—	—	ENP	—
BCA1	P1	BCA2	0.73	4.35	0.91	9.35	15.54	3033	0.834	0.00	0.48	0.44	13.441	0.83	7.7	0.0	BCNP	BCNP
BCA1	P2	BCA17	1.53	−6.56	0.78	—	—	2512	0.615	−0.00	0.72	0.56	—	0.62	11.6	−0.0	BCNP	BCNP
BCA1	P3	BCA3	0.92	2.28	0.72	—	—	3037	0.536	−0.01	0.80	0.59	—	0.54	12.9	−0.1	BCNP	BCNP
BCA1	P4	—	—	—	—	—	—	—	—	—	—	—	—	—	—	—	BCNP	—
BCA10	P1	LOOP2_T	1.23	−3.69	0.93	−0.73	3.63	2737	0.859	0.01	0.31	0.30	2.487	0.86	7.2	0.4	BCNP	BCNP
BCA10	P2	LOOP2_H	1.04	−2.81	0.92	—	—	2722	0.853	0.00	0.33	0.31	—	0.85	7.6	0.2	BCNP	BCNP
BCA10	P3	BCA11	0.70	0.21	0.88	—	—	2795	0.766	−0.01	0.42	0.36	—	0.77	9.7	−0.2	BCNP	BCNP
BCA10	P4	—	—	—	—	—	—	—	—	—	—	—	—	—	—	—	BCNP	—
BCA11	P1	BCA6	0.85	−1.94	0.89	−1.26	4.50	1260	0.772	−0.03	0.45	0.39	3.140	0.78	7.8	−1.1	BCNP	BCNP
BCA11	P2	BCA19	1.04	2.99	0.88	—	—	2101	0.778	−0.02	0.43	0.37	—	0.78	7.4	−0.5	BCNP	BCNP
BCA11	P3	BCA7	0.68	1.98	0.88	—	—	1306	0.781	−0.03	0.44	0.39	—	0.78	7.6	−1.0	BCNP	BCNP
BCA11	P4	—	—	—	—	—	—	—	—	—	—	—	—	—	—	—	BCNP	—

Appendix 3. EDEN water-level estimation equations and performance statistics sorted by station name.—Continued

[n, number of data points; R², coefficient of determination; RMSE, root mean square error; WCA, Water Conservation Area; ENP, Everglades National Park; BCNP, Big Cypress National Preserve; FB, Florida Bay]

[a]Station name	[a]Predictor number	Predictor station name	Slope, m	y-intercept, b	Pearson correlation coefficient	[a]Minimum observed	[a]Maximum observed	n	R²	Mean error	RMSE	Standard error	[a]Average measured, in feet	Nash-Sutcliffe	Percent model error	Percent model bias	Area of site	Area of predictor
BCA12	P1	BCA13	0.93	2.30	0.91	10.29	14.63	2725	0.819	-0.01	0.33	0.29	12.649	0.82	7.5	-0.1	BCNP	BCNP
BCA12	P2	BCA16	1.01	1.71	0.90	—	—	2237	0.804	-0.01	0.34	0.30	—	0.80	7.9	-0.1	BCNP	BCNP
BCA12	P3	L28_GAP	0.91	3.09	0.88	—	—	2593	0.769	-0.01	0.37	0.32	—	0.77	8.5	-0.1	BCNP	BCNP
BCA12	P4	—	—	—	—	—	—	—	—	—	—	—	—	—	—	—	BCNP	—
BCA13	P1	BCA12	0.89	-0.19	0.91	7.52	12.30	2725	0.819	0.01	0.31	0.29	10.860	0.83	6.6	0.1	BCNP	BCNP
BCA13	P2	L28_GAP	1.04	0.15	0.90	—	—	2783	0.786	0.01	0.44	0.40	—	0.79	9.2	0.1	BCNP	BCNP
BCA13	P3	BCA16	1.06	-0.42	0.87	—	—	2398	0.746	0.00	0.48	0.43	—	0.75	10.1	0.0	BCNP	BCNP
BCA13	P4	—	—	—	—	—	—	—	—	—	—	—	—	—	—	—	BCNP	—
BCA14	P1	BCA16	1.25	-5.00	0.89	5.03	9.98	2127	0.792	-0.02	0.49	0.43	8.343	0.80	10.0	-0.2	BCNP	BCNP
BCA14	P2	BCA13	1.11	-3.80	0.86	—	—	2705	0.749	-0.01	0.60	0.51	—	0.75	12.1	-0.2	BCNP	BCNP
BCA14	P3	BCA11	1.10	4.72	0.88	—	—	2407	0.769	-0.01	0.58	0.50	—	0.77	11.8	-0.1	BCNP	BCNP
BCA14	P4	—	—	—	—	—	—	—	—	—	—	—	—	—	—	—	BCNP	—
BCA15	P1	BCA4	0.45	6.77	0.89	9.30	11.33	2487	0.800	0.00	0.22	0.20	10.256	0.80	11.1	0.0	BCNP	BCNP
BCA15	P2	BCA5	0.61	5.01	0.89	—	—	2364	0.788	0.00	0.23	0.21	—	0.79	11.4	0.0	BCNP	BCNP
BCA15	P3	S140_T	0.43	6.17	0.88	—	—	1812	0.776	-0.00	0.23	0.21	—	0.78	11.5	-0.0	BCNP	WCA 3A
BCA15	P4	—	—	—	—	—	—	—	—	—	—	—	—	—	—	—	BCNP	—
BCA16	P1	BCA12	0.81	0.64	0.90	8.11	12.16	2237	0.804	0.01	0.30	0.28	10.780	0.81	7.4	0.1	BCNP	BCNP
BCA16	P2	BCA14	0.64	5.37	0.89	—	—	2127	0.792	0.01	0.35	0.31	—	0.79	8.5	0.1	BCNP	BCNP
BCA16	P3	BCA4	0.68	5.58	0.89	—	—	2429	0.794	0.00	0.37	0.33	—	0.79	9.1	0.0	BCNP	BCNP
BCA16	P4	—	—	—	—	—	—	—	—	—	—	—	—	—	—	—	BCNP	—
BCA17	P1	BCA12	0.62	5.28	0.83	12.04	14.46	2255	0.674	-0.00	0.33	0.28	13.083	0.68	13.6	-0.0	BCNP	BCNP
BCA17	P2	BCA18	0.52	6.74	0.81	—	—	2341	0.654	-0.01	0.35	0.28	—	0.65	14.5	-0.1	BCNP	BCNP
BCA17	P3	BCA2	0.35	8.77	0.81	—	—	2433	0.651	0.00	0.34	0.27	—	0.65	14.0	-0.0	BCNP	BCNP
BCA17	P4	—	—	—	—	—	—	—	—	—	—	—	—	—	—	—	BCNP	—
BCA18	P1	BCA5	1.06	3.17	0.90	8.37	13.68	2341	0.807	0.00	0.42	0.38	12.225	0.81	7.9	0.0	BCNP	BCNP
BCA18	P2	L28_GAP	0.95	2.36	0.89	—	—	2224	0.798	0.00	0.41	0.38	—	0.80	7.8	0.0	BCNP	BCNP
BCA18	P3	BCA12	0.96	0.21	0.86	—	—	2223	0.727	0.01	0.44	0.39	—	0.73	8.4	0.1	BCNP	BCNP
BCA18	P4	S190_T	1.07	1.88	0.87	—	—	2470	0.734	-0.02	0.49	0.44	—	0.73	9.2	-0.2	BCNP	L28 Interceptor Canal
BCA19	P1	BCA8	0.78	-0.28	0.95	-1.74	1.78	2314	0.899	-0.00	0.24	0.23	0.347	0.90	6.9	-0.5	BCNP	BCNP
BCA19	P2	BCA7	0.60	-0.85	0.92	—	—	1297	0.835	-0.00	0.30	0.29	—	0.83	8.7	-1.2	BCNP	BCNP
BCA19	P3	BCA6	0.72	-4.12	0.91	—	—	1251	0.805	-0.01	0.33	0.30	—	0.81	9.4	-2.0	BCNP	BCNP
BCA19	P4	—	—	—	—	—	—	—	—	—	—	—	—	—	—	—	BCNP	—
BCA2	P1	BCA1	1.14	-2.88	0.91	7.42	14.77	3033	0.834	-0.00	0.60	0.55	12.441	0.83	8.1	-0.0	BCNP	BCNP
BCA2	P2	BCA3	1.31	-3.49	0.84	—	—	2995	0.725	-0.02	0.76	0.65	—	0.73	10.4	-0.2	BCNP	BCNP
BCA2	P3	BCA18	1.15	-1.42	0.80	—	—	2415	0.602	-0.09	0.84	0.61	—	0.61	11.4	-0.7	BCNP	BCNP
BCA2	P4	—	—	—	—	—	—	—	—	—	—	—	—	—	—	—	BCNP	—

Appendix 3. EDEN water-level estimation equations and performance statistics sorted by station name.—Continued

[n, number of data points; R², coefficient of determination; RMSE, root mean square error; WCA, Water Conservation Area; ENP, Everglades National Park; BCNP, Big Cypress National Preserve; FB, Florida Bay]

Station name [a]	Predictor number [a]	Predictor station name	Slope, m	y-intercept, b	Pearson correlation coefficient	Minimum observed [a]	Maximum observed [a]	n	R²	Mean error	RMSE	Standard error	Average measured, in feet [a]	Nash-Sutcliffe	Percent model error	Percent model bias	Area of site	Area of predictor
BCA20	P1	LOOP1_T	0.90	-1.57	0.91	0.86	5.20	2426	0.819	-0.01	0.26	0.23	3.934	0.82	5.9	-0.2	BCNP	BCNP
BCA20	P2	LOOP2_H	0.61	0.86	0.90	—	—	2436	0.812	-0.02	0.27	0.23	—	0.81	6.1	-0.5	BCNP	BCNP
BCA20	P3	LOOP2_T	0.66	0.71	0.87	—	—	2389	0.766	-0.02	0.26	0.22	—	0.76	6.0	-0.5	BCNP	BCNP
BCA20	P4	—	—	—	—	—	—	—	—	—	—	—	—	—	—	—	BCNP	—
BCA3	P1	BCA18	0.68	3.92	0.86	8.10	13.58	2411	0.671	-0.04	0.47	0.37	12.128	0.67	8.7	-0.3	BCNP	BCNP
BCA3	P2	BCA2	0.54	5.39	0.84	—	—	2995	0.725	0.00	0.49	0.41	—	0.73	9.0	0.0	BCNP	BCNP
BCA3	P3	BCA13	0.71	4.40	0.79	—	—	3025	0.613	-0.03	0.59	0.44	—	0.61	10.7	-0.2	BCNP	BCNP
BCA3	P4	—	—	—	—	—	—	—	—	—	—	—	—	—	—	—	BCNP	—
BCA4	P1	BCA15	1.77	-10.45	0.89	5.04	9.24	2487	0.800	-0.00	0.44	0.40	7.563	0.80	10.6	-0.0	BCNP	BCNP
BCA4	P2	BCA16	1.17	-4.94	0.89	—	—	2429	0.794	0.00	0.48	0.43	—	0.79	11.5	0.0	BCNP	BCNP
BCA4	P3	BCA19	1.22	7.18	0.89	—	—	2367	0.798	-0.00	0.48	0.42	—	0.80	11.3	-0.0	BCNP	BCNP
BCA4	P4	—	—	—	—	—	—	—	—	—	—	—	—	—	—	—	BCNP	—
BCA5	P1	BCA16	0.91	-1.24	0.90	6.21	9.80	2382	0.817	-0.00	0.35	0.32	8.504	0.82	9.8	-0.0	BCNP	BCNP
BCA5	P2	BCA18	0.76	-0.70	0.90	—	—	2341	0.807	-0.01	0.36	0.32	—	0.81	10.0	-0.1	BCNP	BCNP
BCA5	P3	BCA6	0.79	3.58	0.89	—	—	1189	0.763	-0.03	0.43	0.37	—	0.76	11.9	-0.3	BCNP	BCNP
BCA5	P4	—	—	—	—	—	—	—	—	—	—	—	—	—	—	—	BCNP	—
BCA6	P1	LOOP2_H	1.16	0.29	0.93	2.93	7.56	969	0.775	0.07	0.51	0.49	6.235	0.75	10.9	1.1	BCNP	BCNP
BCA6	P2	LOOP2_T	1.37	-0.63	0.92	—	—	1027	0.726	0.07	0.52	0.51	—	0.68	11.3	1.1	BCNP	BCNP
BCA6	P3	LOOP1_T	1.52	-3.11	0.91	—	—	1009	0.655	0.10	0.56	0.54	—	0.56	12.0	1.6	BCNP	BCNP
BCA6	P4	BCA19	1.14	5.82	0.91	—	—	1251	0.805	0.01	0.42	0.38	—	0.80	9.0	0.2	BCNP	BCNP
BCA7	P1	BCA8	1.23	1.01	0.98	-2.01	4.30	1289	0.960	0.00	0.23	0.22	1.969	0.96	3.6	0.1	BCNP	BCNP
BCA7	P2	BCA19	1.41	1.50	0.92	—	—	1297	0.835	0.01	0.48	0.43	—	0.83	7.6	0.4	BCNP	BCNP
BCA7	P3	BCA13	1.00	-8.87	0.89	—	—	1220	0.778	0.01	0.56	0.48	—	0.78	8.9	0.8	BCNP	BCNP
BCA7	P4	—	—	—	—	—	—	—	—	—	—	—	—	—	—	—	BCNP	—
BCA8	P1	BCA7	0.78	-0.75	0.98	-1.67	2.48	1289	0.960	-0.00	0.18	0.18	0.734	0.96	4.4	-0.2	BCNP	BCNP
BCA8	P2	BCA19	1.16	0.41	0.95	—	—	2314	0.899	0.00	0.30	0.28	—	0.90	7.2	0.3	BCNP	BCNP
BCA8	P3	BCA16	1.06	-10.62	0.90	—	—	2409	0.794	0.01	0.44	0.39	—	0.80	10.5	1.8	BCNP	BCNP
BCA8	P4	—	—	—	—	—	—	—	—	—	—	—	—	—	—	—	BCNP	—
BCA9	P1	LOOP2_H	0.89	0.97	0.94	3.03	6.88	2735	0.887	-0.01	0.25	0.24	5.458	0.89	6.5	-0.1	BCNP	BCNP
BCA9	P2	LOOP1_T	1.35	-2.85	0.94	—	—	2767	0.880	0.01	0.26	0.25	—	0.88	6.6	0.2	BCNP	BCNP
BCA9	P3	LOOP1_H	1.32	-2.65	0.94	—	—	2846	0.882	0.00	0.24	0.23	—	0.88	6.2	0.1	BCNP	BCNP
BCA9	P4	NP205	0.72	2.13	0.90	—	—	3113	0.809	0.01	0.32	0.29	—	0.81	8.3	0.2	BCNP	ENP

Appendix 3. EDEN water-level estimation equations and performance statistics sorted by station name.—Continued

[n, number of data points; R^2, coefficient of determination; RMSE, root mean square error; WCA, Water Conservation Area; ENP, Everglades National Park; BCNP, Big Cypress National Preserve; FB, Florida Bay]

[a]Station name	[a]Predictor number	Predictor station name	Slope, m	y-intercept, b	Pearson correlation coefficient	[a]Minimum observed	[a]Maximum observed	n	R^2	Mean error	RMSE	Standard error	[a]Average measured, in feet	Nash-Sutcliffe	Percent model error	Percent model bias	Area of site	Area of predictor
C111_wetland_east_of_FIU_LTER_TSPH5	P1	EVER8	0.65	-0.04	0.93	0.06	1.58	803	0.863	-0.01	0.09	0.06	0.493	0.83	6.0	-2.1	ENP	ENP
C111_wetland_east_of_FIU_LTER_TSPH5	P2	EVER7	0.67	-0.11	0.90	—	—	803	0.847	-0.01	0.10	0.06	—	0.80	6.4	-1.6	ENP	ENP
C111_wetland_east_of_FIU_LTER_TSPH5	P3	CT50R	0.63	0.07	0.90	—	—	803	0.915	-0.01	0.10	0.04	—	0.80	6.5	-3.0	ENP	ENP
C111_wetland_east_of_FIU_LTER_TSPH5	P4	—	—	—	—	—	—	—	—	—	—	—	—	—	—	—	ENP	—
CP	P1	NCL	0.94	-0.07	0.99	-2.14	1.32	3014	0.978	0.00	0.09	0.09	-0.327	0.98	2.5	-0.1	ENP	ENP
CP	P2	E146	1.16	0.13	0.97	—	—	3084	0.934	-0.00	0.15	0.15	—	0.93	4.4	0.0	ENP	ENP
CP	P3	Taylor_Slough_wetland_at_E146	1.12	0.00	0.95	—	—	1023	0.907	0.00	0.13	0.12	—	0.94	3.7	-0.0	ENP	ENP
CP	P4	—	—	—	—	—	—	—	—	—	—	—	—	—	—	—	ENP	—
CR2	P1	RG2	1.03	-0.21	0.98	0.44	5.44	3091	0.969	-0.00	0.20	0.20	3.548	0.97	4.0	-0.0	ENP	ENP
CR2	P2	CR3	1.01	-0.01	0.98	—	—	3118	0.966	0.00	0.21	0.21	—	0.97	4.2	0.0	ENP	ENP
CR2	P3	NTS10	0.96	0.69	0.97	—	—	3117	0.950	-0.00	0.25	0.25	—	0.95	5.1	-0.0	ENP	ENP
CR2	P4	—	—	—	—	—	—	—	—	—	—	—	—	—	—	—	ENP	—
CR3	P1	CR2	0.95	0.13	0.98	0.06	5.34	3118	0.966	-0.00	0.20	0.20	3.512	0.97	3.8	-0.0	ENP	ENP
CR3	P2	NP206	1.05	-0.70	0.98	—	—	3155	0.958	0.00	0.22	0.22	—	0.96	4.3	0.0	ENP	ENP
CR3	P3	A13	1.11	0.31	0.97	—	—	3155	0.935	0.00	0.28	0.27	—	0.94	5.3	0.0	ENP	ENP
CR3	P4	—	—	—	—	—	—	—	—	—	—	—	—	—	—	—	ENP	—

Appendix 3. EDEN water-level estimation equations and performance statistics sorted by station name.—Continued

[n, number of data points; R², coefficient of determination; RMSE, root mean square error; WCA, Water Conservation Area; ENP, Everglades National Park; BCNP, Big Cypress National Preserve; FB, Florida Bay]

Station name	Predictor number	Predictor station name	Slope, m	y-intercept, b	Pearson correlation coefficient	Minimum observed	Maximum observed	n	R²	Mean error	RMSE	Standard error	Average measured, in feet	Nash-Sutcliffe	Percent model error	Percent model bias	Area of site	Area of predictor
CT27R	P1	CT50R	1.00	0.19	0.99	−0.55	1.72	3071	0.986	−0.00	0.06	0.06	0.484	0.99	2.5	−0.0	ENP	ENP
CT27R	P2	EVER6	1.11	−0.04	0.98	—	—	3090	0.971	−0.00	0.08	0.08	—	0.97	3.6	−0.3	ENP	ENP
CT27R	P3	CV5NR	0.79	0.18	0.89	—	—	3110	0.787	0.00	0.22	0.20	—	0.79	9.9	0.0	ENP	ENP
CT27R	P4	—	—	—	—	—	—	—	—	—	—	—	—	—	—	—	ENP	—
CT50R	P1	S18C_T	0.96	−1.53	1.00	−1.03	1.35	2991	0.993	−0.00	0.04	0.04	0.288	0.99	1.7	−0.0	ENP	C111 Canal
CT50R	P2	CT27R	0.99	−0.18	0.99	—	—	3071	0.986	−0.00	0.06	0.06	—	0.99	2.4	−0.0	ENP	ENP
CT50R	P3	EVER6	1.10	−0.22	0.99	—	—	3077	0.978	−0.00	0.07	0.07	—	0.98	3.0	−0.5	ENP	ENP
CT50R	P4	—	—	—	—	—	—	—	—	—	—	—	—	—	—	—	ENP	—
CV5NR	P1	CT27R	0.99	−0.10	0.89	−1.45	4.69	3110	0.787	−0.00	0.25	0.22	0.371	0.79	4.1	−0.0	ENP	ENP
CV5NR	P2	EVER6	1.11	−0.13	0.89	—	—	3129	0.788	−0.00	0.25	0.22	—	0.79	4.1	−0.4	ENP	ENP
CV5NR	P3	CT50R	1.01	0.09	0.90	—	—	3099	0.802	−0.00	0.24	0.22	—	0.80	4.0	−0.0	ENP	ENP
CV5NR	P4	—	—	—	—	—	—	—	—	—	—	—	—	—	—	—	ENP	—
CY2	P1	CY3	0.92	0.14	0.98	−1.83	1.93	3148	0.960	−0.00	0.15	0.14	0.585	0.96	3.9	−0.0	ENP	ENP
CY2	P2	DO1	0.74	−0.14	0.97	—	—	3148	0.935	−0.00	0.19	0.18	—	0.93	5.0	−0.0	ENP	ENP
CY2	P3	NP67	1.02	0.03	0.92	—	—	3109	0.857	−0.00	0.28	0.25	—	0.86	7.4	−0.7	ENP	ENP
CY2	P4	—	—	—	—	—	—	—	—	—	—	—	—	—	—	—	ENP	—
CY3	P1	CY2	1.04	−0.13	0.98	−2.09	2.05	3148	0.960	0.00	0.16	0.15	0.485	0.96	3.8	0.0	ENP	ENP
CY3	P2	DO2	0.78	−0.47	0.98	—	—	3155	0.956	−0.00	0.16	0.16	—	0.96	4.0	−0.0	ENP	ENP
CY3	P3	NP46	1.11	0.60	0.95	—	—	3143	0.946	−0.01	0.18	0.17	—	0.95	4.4	−2.0	ENP	ENP
CY3	P4	—	—	—	—	—	—	—	—	—	—	—	—	—	—	—	ENP	—
DO1	P1	DO2	0.97	−0.21	0.99	−1.80	3.05	3155	0.982	0.00	0.13	0.13	0.978	0.98	2.7	0.0	ENP	ENP
DO1	P2	NP72	0.80	−0.11	0.98	—	—	3131	0.960	−0.00	0.19	0.19	—	0.96	3.9	−0.1	ENP	ENP
DO1	P3	CY3	1.20	0.40	0.98	—	—	3155	0.954	0.00	0.21	0.20	—	0.95	4.3	0.0	ENP	ENP
DO1	P4	—	—	—	—	—	—	—	—	—	—	—	—	—	—	—	ENP	—
DO2	P1	DO1	1.01	0.24	0.99	−1.73	3.41	3155	0.982	−0.00	0.13	0.13	1.228	0.98	2.6	−0.0	ENP	ENP
DO2	P2	NP44	0.75	−0.16	0.98	—	—	3153	0.963	−0.00	0.19	0.18	—	0.96	3.7	−0.2	ENP	ENP
DO2	P3	NP72	0.82	0.12	0.98	—	—	3131	0.955	−0.00	0.21	0.20	—	0.95	4.0	−0.1	ENP	ENP
DO2	P4	—	—	—	—	—	—	—	—	—	—	—	—	—	—	—	ENP	—
E112	P1	TSB	0.98	0.78	0.99	−0.26	4.56	1799	0.979	0.00	0.16	0.16	2.486	0.98	3.4	0.0	ENP	ENP
E112	P2	NTS1	0.98	−0.21	0.98	—	—	3129	0.968	−0.00	0.20	0.19	—	0.97	4.1	−0.0	ENP	ENP
E112	P3	L31W	0.98	−0.22	0.97	—	—	3037	0.943	−0.00	0.27	0.26	—	0.94	5.5	−0.0	ENP	ENP
E112	P4	—	—	—	—	—	—	—	—	—	—	—	—	—	—	—	ENP	—

Appendix 3. EDEN water-level estimation equations and performance statistics sorted by station name.—Continued

[n, number of data points; R^2, coefficient of determination; RMSE, root mean square error; WCA, Water Conservation Area; ENP, Everglades National Park; BCNP, Big Cypress National Preserve; FB, Florida Bay]

[a]Station name	[a]Predictor number	Predictor station name	Slope, m	y-intercept, b	Pearson correlation coefficient	[a]Minimum observed	[a]Maximum observed	n	R^2	Mean error	RMSE	Standard error	[a]Average measured, in feet	Nash-Sutcliffe	Percent model error	Percent model bias	Area of site	Area of predictor
E146	P1	Taylor_Slough_wetland_at_E146	0.95	-0.10	0.99	-2.12	1.00	1030	0.989	-0.00	0.04	0.04	-0.405	0.99	1.1	0.0	ENP	ENP
E146	P2	CP	0.81	-0.13	0.97	—	—	3084	0.934	0.00	0.13	0.12	—	0.93	4.1	-0.0	ENP	ENP
E146	P3	P37	0.87	-0.32	0.97	—	—	3121	0.935	0.00	0.13	0.13	—	0.94	4.2	-0.0	ENP	ENP
E146	P4	—	—	—	—	—	—	—	—	—	—	—	—	—	—	—	ENP	—
EDEN_1	P1	LOOP1_T	0.85	1.95	0.90	7.11	8.13	482	0.640	0.01	0.11	0.11	7.333	0.59	11.1	0.2	BCNP	BCNP
EDEN_1	P2	S343A_T	0.50	3.80	0.83	—	—	393	0.748	-0.00	0.08	0.07	—	0.75	8.3	-0.0	BCNP	L28 Canal
EDEN_1	P3	S344_T	0.26	5.25	0.70	—	—	350	0.533	0.00	0.11	0.07	—	0.55	10.5	0.0	BCNP	BCNP
EDEN_1	P4	—	—	—	—	—	—	—	—	—	—	—	—	—	—	—	BCNP	—
EDEN_10	P1	SRS1	0.74	0.44	0.97	4.81	6.60	801	0.936	-0.00	0.09	0.09	5.717	0.94	5.0	-0.0	WCA 3B	WCA 3B
EDEN_10	P2	TI-8	0.82	1.32	0.97	—	—	801	0.936	-0.00	0.09	0.09	—	0.94	5.0	-0.0	WCA 3B	WCA 3B
EDEN_10	P3	TI-9	1.24	-1.58	0.94	—	—	801	0.878	0.00	0.12	0.12	—	0.88	6.9	0.0	WCA 3B	WCA 3B
EDEN_10	P4	—	—	—	—	—	—	—	—	—	—	—	—	—	—	—	WCA 3B	—
EDEN_11	P1	G339_T	0.34	7.27	0.85	10.59	13.16	798	0.718	0.00	0.28	0.23	11.356	0.72	10.8	0.0	WCA 2A	L6 Canal
EDEN_11	P2	S7_T	0.33	7.81	0.84	—	—	799	0.716	0.00	0.28	0.23	—	0.72	10.8	0.0	WCA 2A	L38E Canal
EDEN_11	P3	S10D_T	0.50	4.90	0.81	—	—	739	0.649	-0.00	0.32	0.26	—	0.65	12.3	-0.0	WCA 2A	WCA 2A
EDEN_11	P4	—	—	—	—	—	—	—	—	—	—	—	—	—	—	—	WCA 2A	—
EDEN_12	P1	S151_H	0.95	0.46	0.99	6.11	9.69	714	0.967	0.01	0.14	0.14	7.767	0.97	3.8	0.1	WCA 3A	Miami Canal
EDEN_12	P2	EDEN_4	0.86	0.95	0.98	—	—	782	0.968	-0.00	0.14	0.14	—	0.97	3.8	-0.0	WCA 3A	WCA 3A
EDEN_12	P3	W14	1.24	-1.96	0.98	—	—	708	0.965	-0.00	0.13	0.13	—	0.97	3.6	-0.0	WCA 3A	WCA 3A
EDEN_12	P4	—	—	—	—	—	—	—	—	—	—	—	—	—	—	—	WCA 3A	—
EDEN_13	P1	S146_H	0.73	0.71	0.92	6.98	9.49	573	0.855	-0.00	0.25	0.23	7.894	0.85	9.9	-0.0	WCA 2B	WCA 2A
EDEN_13	P2	SITE_17	0.78	-1.68	0.89	—	—	745	0.793	0.00	0.28	0.25	—	0.79	11.1	0.0	WCA 2B	WCA 2A
EDEN_13	P3	SITE_99	0.50	3.33	0.87	—	—	740	0.761	0.00	0.30	0.26	—	0.76	11.9	0.0	WCA 2B	WCA 2B
EDEN_13	P4	—	—	—	—	—	—	—	—	—	—	—	—	—	—	—	WCA 2B	—
EDEN_14	P1	3A-5	1.03	-0.29	0.98	8.21	10.01	668	0.955	0.00	0.09	0.09	8.733	0.96	5.2	0.0	WCA 3A	WCA 3A
EDEN_14	P2	W18	0.97	0.57	0.97	—	—	647	0.950	0.00	0.10	0.10	—	0.95	5.5	0.0	WCA 3A	WCA 3A
EDEN_14	P3	3AS	0.97	0.22	0.97	—	—	678	0.934	-0.00	0.12	0.11	—	0.93	6.4	-0.0	WCA 3A	WCA 3A
EDEN_14	P4	—	—	—	—	—	—	—	—	—	—	—	—	—	—	—	WCA 3A	—
EDEN_3	P1	OT	0.65	-0.11	0.95	-0.64	1.09	899	0.893	-0.00	0.12	0.11	0.233	0.89	7.1	-1.4	ENP	ENP
EDEN_3	P2	P34	0.62	-0.49	0.90	—	—	959	0.813	0.00	0.17	0.15	—	0.81	9.7	0.0	ENP	ENP
EDEN_3	P3	P36	0.89	-2.12	0.89	—	—	972	0.787	0.00	0.18	0.16	—	0.79	10.3	0.0	ENP	ENP
EDEN_3	P4	—	—	—	—	—	—	—	—	—	—	—	—	—	—	—	ENP	—

Appendix 3. EDEN water-level estimation equations and performance statistics sorted by station name.—Continued

[n, number of data points; R², coefficient of determination; RMSE, root mean square error; WCA, Water Conservation Area; ENP, Everglades National Park; BCNP, Big Cypress National Preserve; FB, Florida Bay]

Station name	Predictor number	Predictor station name	Slope, m	y-intercept, b	Pearson correlation coefficient	Minimum observed	Maximum observed	n	R²	Mean error	RMSE	Standard error	Average measured, in feet	Nash-Sutcliffe	Percent model error	Percent model bias	Area of site	Area of predictor
EDEN_4	P1	S151_H	1.10	-0.53	0.99	6.27	10.32	711	0.973	0.01	0.14	0.14	7.978	0.97	3.5	0.1	WCA 3A	Miami Canal
EDEN_4	P2	EDEN_12	1.13	-0.80	0.98	—	—	782	0.968	0.00	0.16	0.15	—	0.97	3.9	0.0	WCA 3A	WCA 3A
EDEN_4	P3	S9A_T	0.98	0.25	0.98	—	—	796	0.964	-0.00	0.17	0.16	—	0.96	4.1	-0.0	WCA 3A	WCA 3B
EDEN_4	P4	—	—	—	—	—	—	—	—	—	—	—	—	—	—	—	WCA 3A	—
EDEN_5	P1	3A9	0.80	1.70	0.97	8.06	10.26	677	0.935	0.00	0.12	0.12	8.925	0.94	5.4	0.0	WCA 3A	WCA 3A
EDEN_5	P2	3AN1W1	0.94	0.05	0.96	—	—	674	0.932	0.00	0.12	0.12	—	0.93	5.6	0.0	WCA 3A	WCA 3A
EDEN_5	P3	SITE_62	0.87	-0.56	0.96	—	—	674	0.928	0.00	0.13	0.12	—	0.93	5.7	0.0	WCA 3A	WCA 3A
EDEN_5	P4	—	—	—	—	—	—	—	—	—	—	—	—	—	—	—	WCA 3A	—
EDEN_6	P1	BCA5	0.67	3.87	0.89	8.54	10.72	649	0.835	0.00	0.19	0.18	9.573	0.84	8.7	0.0	BCNP	BCNP
EDEN_6	P2	EDEN_5	0.96	1.00	0.91	—	—	652	0.822	0.00	0.20	0.18	—	0.82	9.2	0.0	BCNP	WCA 3A
EDEN_6	P3	L28S2	0.85	1.50	0.90	—	—	711	0.644	0.04	0.29	0.24	—	0.64	13.2	0.4	BCNP	L28 Canal
EDEN_6	P4	—	—	—	—	—	—	—	—	—	—	—	—	—	—	—	BCNP	—
EDEN_7	P1	S151_T	0.81	0.99	0.96	5.02	7.01	794	0.911	0.01	0.12	0.11	5.796	0.91	5.9	0.1	WCA 3B	Miami Canal
EDEN_7	P2	SITE_76	1.05	-1.96	0.96	—	—	764	0.914	-0.00	0.12	0.11	—	0.91	5.9	-0.0	WCA 3B	WCA 3B
EDEN_7	P3	S31_H	0.79	1.26	0.95	—	—	803	0.898	0.00	0.13	0.12	—	0.90	6.3	0.0	WCA 3B	Miami Canal
EDEN_7	P4	—	—	—	—	—	—	—	—	—	—	—	—	—	—	—	WCA 3B	—
EDEN_8	P1	SITE_65	1.12	-2.56	0.99	6.55	9.19	801	0.990	0.00	0.06	0.06	7.841	0.99	2.2	0.0	WCA 3A	WCA 3A
EDEN_8	P2	W5	1.07	-0.42	0.99	—	—	785	0.982	0.00	0.07	0.07	—	0.98	2.8	0.0	WCA 3A	WCA 3A
EDEN_8	P3	W14	0.94	0.49	0.99	—	—	728	0.974	-0.00	0.08	0.08	—	0.98	3.1	-0.0	WCA 3A	WCA 3A
EDEN_8	P4	—	—	—	—	—	—	—	—	—	—	—	—	—	—	—	WCA 3A	—
EDEN_9	P1	S150_T	0.75	2.38	0.98	7.70	10.45	528	0.565	-0.19	0.53	0.50	8.614	0.27	19.4	-2.2	WCA 3A	WCA 3A
EDEN_9	P2	3ANE	0.94	0.14	0.96	—	—	613	0.923	-0.00	0.16	0.16	—	0.92	6.0	-0.0	WCA 3A	WCA 3A
EDEN_9	P3	3A9	1.11	-1.47	0.95	—	—	629	0.906	0.00	0.18	0.17	—	0.91	6.6	0.0	WCA 3A	WCA 3A
EDEN_9	P4	—	—	—	—	—	—	—	—	—	—	—	—	—	—	—	WCA 3A	—
EPSW	P1	EVER6	0.71	-0.37	0.97	-0.94	0.98	3032	0.948	0.00	0.07	0.07	-0.038	0.95	3.8	-0.7	ENP	ENP
EPSW	P2	CT50R	0.64	-0.23	0.96	—	—	3002	0.921	0.00	0.09	0.09	—	0.92	4.6	-6.3	ENP	ENP
EPSW	P3	CT27R	0.62	-0.34	0.95	—	—	3013	0.900	0.00	0.10	0.09	—	0.90	5.1	-6.4	ENP	ENP
EPSW	P4	—	—	—	—	—	—	—	—	—	—	—	—	—	—	—	ENP	—
EVER4	P1	EVER7	1.03	1.40	0.96	0.46	3.24	2936	0.913	-0.00	0.12	0.12	1.993	0.91	4.5	-0.0	ENP	ENP
EVER4	P2	R127	0.70	1.53	0.96	—	—	3052	0.933	0.00	0.12	0.12	—	0.93	4.4	0.1	ENP	ENP
EVER4	P3	CT50R	0.94	1.71	0.95	—	—	3030	0.903	-0.00	0.15	0.14	—	0.90	5.3	-0.0	ENP	ENP
EVER4	P4	—	—	—	—	—	—	—	—	—	—	—	—	—	—	—	ENP	—

Appendix 3. EDEN water-level estimation equations and performance statistics sorted by station name.—Continued

[n, number of data points; R², coefficient of determination; RMSE, root mean square error; WCA, Water Conservation Area; ENP, Everglades National Park; BCNP, Big Cypress National Preserve; FB, Florida Bay]

[a]Station name	[a]Predictor number	Predictor station name	Slope, m	y-intercept, b	Pearson correlation coefficient	[a]Minimum observed	[a]Maximum observed	n	R²	Mean error	RMSE	Standard error	[a]Average measured, in feet	Nash-Sutcliffe	Percent model error	Percent model bias	Area of site	Area of predictor
EVER6	P1	CT50R	0.89	0.21	0.99	−0.98	1.78	3077	0.978	0.00	0.06	0.06	0.464	0.98	2.3	0.3	ENP	ENP
EVER6	P2	CT27R	0.87	0.05	0.98	—	—	3090	0.971	0.00	0.07	0.07	—	0.97	2.6	0.3	ENP	ENP
EVER6	P3	S18C_T	0.85	−1.15	0.98	—	—	3021	0.970	0.00	0.08	0.08	—	0.97	2.8	0.3	ENP	C111 Canal
EVER6	P4	—	—	—	—	—	—	—	—	—	—	—	—	—	—	—	ENP	—
EVER7	P1	CT50R	0.84	0.33	0.96	−0.35	2.00	2944	0.930	−0.00	0.10	0.10	0.618	0.93	4.4	−0.0	ENP	ENP
EVER7	P2	EVER6	0.94	0.14	0.96	—	—	2962	0.924	−0.00	0.11	0.10	—	0.92	4.6	−0.2	ENP	ENP
EVER7	P3	S18C_T	0.80	−0.94	0.95	—	—	2876	0.901	−0.00	0.12	0.12	—	0.90	5.2	−0.0	ENP	C111 Canal
EVER7	P4	—	—	—	—	—	—	—	—	—	—	—	—	—	—	—	ENP	—
EVER8	P1	CT50R	0.95	0.14	0.97	−0.99	1.99	3061	0.950	0.00	0.11	0.10	0.421	0.95	3.5	0.2	ENP	ENP
EVER8	P2	S18C_T	0.91	−1.31	0.97	—	—	2992	0.940	0.00	0.12	0.11	—	0.94	3.9	0.2	ENP	C111 Canal
EVER8	P3	EVER6	1.05	−0.07	0.97	—	—	3097	0.941	−0.00	0.11	0.11	—	0.94	3.8	−0.1	ENP	ENP
EVER8	P4	—	—	—	—	—	—	—	—	—	—	—	—	—	—	—	ENP	—
G119_H	P1	S336_T	0.98	0.31	1.00	2.05	5.51	2555	0.995	−0.00	0.05	0.05	4.137	0.99	1.4	−0.1	Tamiami Canal	Tamiami Canal
G119_H	P2	L31NN	0.64	1.21	0.97	—	—	1067	0.884	−0.05	0.23	0.21	—	0.88	6.7	−1.3	Tamiami Canal	L31N Canal
G119_H	P3	3BS1W1	0.73	0.49	0.95	—	—	2358	0.911	−0.01	0.19	0.18	—	0.91	5.5	−0.2	Tamiami Canal	WCA 3B Canal
G119_H	P4	—	—	—	—	—	—	—	—	—	—	—	—	—	—	—	Tamiami Canal	—
G119_T	P1	S380_H	1.00	0.09	1.00	1.26	5.53	1288	0.993	−0.01	0.05	0.05	2.722	0.99	1.2	−0.5	Tamiami Canal	Pennsuco Wetlands
G119_T	P2	S150_T	0.47	−1.56	0.83	—	—	1004	0.600	−0.01	0.39	0.34	—	0.62	9.2	−0.4	Tamiami Canal	WCA 3A Canal
G119_T	P3	L31W	0.54	1.25	0.82	—	—	2458	0.640	−0.00	0.43	0.36	—	0.64	10.0	−0.1	Tamiami Canal	ENP
G119_T	P4	—	—	—	—	—	—	—	—	—	—	—	—	—	—	—	Tamiami Canal	—
G211_H	P1	L31N_7	0.96	−1.36	0.99	2.12	6.15	3099	0.984	0.00	0.07	0.07	3.975	0.98	1.7	0.0	L31N Canal	L31N Canal
G211_H	P2	L31N_4	0.96	−1.40	0.99	—	—	3114	0.984	0.00	0.07	0.07	—	0.98	1.8	0.0	L31N Canal	L31N Canal
G211_H	P3	L31N_1	0.95	−1.35	0.99	—	—	3109	0.984	0.00	0.07	0.07	—	0.98	1.8	0.0	L31N Canal	L31N Canal
G211_H	P4	—	—	—	—	—	—	—	—	—	—	—	—	—	—	—	L31N Canal	—

Appendix 3. EDEN water-level estimation equations and performance statistics sorted by station name.—Continued

[n, number of data points; R², coefficient of determination; RMSE, root mean square error; WCA, Water Conservation Area; ENP, Everglades National Park; BCNP, Big Cypress National Preserve; FB, Florida Bay]

Station name	Predictor number	Predictor station name	Slope, m	y-intercept, b	Pearson correlation coefficient	Minimum observed	Maximum observed	n	R²	Mean error	RMSE	Standard error	Average measured, in feet	Nash-Sutcliffe	Percent model error	Percent model bias	Area of site	Area of predictor
G211_T	P1	TI-9	0.42	0.55	0.33	1.96	6.76	941	0.109	0.00	0.33	0.11	3.069	0.14	6.8	0.0	L31N Canal	WCA 3B
G211_T	P2	TI-8	0.26	1.61	0.31	—	—	941	0.097	0.00	0.33	0.10	—	0.13	6.8	0.0	L31N Canal	WCA 3B
G211_T	P3	S336_H	0.21	2.30	0.28	—	—	3049	0.081	0.00	0.42	0.12	—	0.08	8.7	0.0	L31N Canal	Tamiami Canal
G211_T	P4	—	—	—	—	—	—	—	—	—	—	—	—	—	—	—	L31N Canal	—
G300_T	P1	SITE_8C	1.02	-2.14	0.99	10.33	16.35	2961	0.985	0.00	0.11	0.11	14.447	0.98	1.9	0.0	L40 Canal	WCA 1
G300_T	P2	G301_T	1.01	-0.29	0.99	—	—	3054	0.983	0.00	0.12	0.12	—	0.98	2.0	0.0	L40 Canal	L7 Canal
G300_T	P3	S10D_H	1.04	-2.21	0.98	—	—	3030	0.959	0.00	0.18	0.17	—	0.96	2.9	0.0	L40 Canal	L39 Canal
G300_T	P4	—	—	—	—	—	—	—	—	—	—	—	—	—	—	—	L40 Canal	—
G301_T	P1	G300_T	0.98	0.53	0.99	10.47	16.55	3054	0.983	-0.00	0.12	0.11	14.616	0.98	1.9	-0.0	L7 Canal	L40 Canal
G301_T	P2	SITE_8C	1.00	-1.62	0.99	—	—	3060	0.978	0.00	0.14	0.13	—	0.98	2.2	0.0	L7 Canal	WCA 1
G301_T	P3	S10D_H	1.02	-1.74	0.98	—	—	3128	0.962	0.00	0.17	0.17	—	0.96	2.8	0.0	L7 Canal	L39 Canal
G301_T	P4	—	—	—	—	—	—	—	—	—	—	—	—	—	—	—	L7 Canal	—
G339_H	P1	G339_T	0.60	5.01	0.58	9.58	16.54	2375	0.340	0.00	0.97	0.57	12.351	0.34	14.0	0.0	L6 Canal	L6 Canal
G339_H	P2	EDEN_11	1.28	-2.11	0.54	—	—	796	0.296	0.00	1.03	0.56	—	0.30	14.9	0.0	L6 Canal	WCA 2A
G339_H	P3	S7_T	0.43	7.72	0.47	—	—	2534	0.220	0.00	1.10	0.51	—	0.22	15.8	0.0	L6 Canal	L38E Canal
G339_H	P4	—	—	—	—	—	—	—	—	—	—	—	—	—	—	—	L6 Canal	—
G339_T	P1	EDEN_11	2.13	-12.05	0.85	9.94	15.82	798	0.718	0.00	0.70	0.59	12.421	0.73	11.9	0.0	L6 Canal	WCA 2A
G339_T	P2	S339_H	1.15	1.08	0.77	—	—	2359	0.598	0.00	0.76	0.59	—	0.60	12.9	0.0	L6 Canal	Miami Canal
G339_T	P3	S7_T	0.67	5.20	0.75	—	—	2524	0.568	0.00	0.77	0.58	—	0.57	13.2	0.0	L6 Canal	L38E Canal
G339_T	P4	—	—	—	—	—	—	—	—	—	—	—	—	—	—	—	L6 Canal	—
Joe_Bay_2E	P1	Trout_Creek_at_mouth	1.04	0.12	0.94	-1.41	1.55	1359	0.884	-0.00	0.14	0.13	-0.464	0.88	4.7	0.1	Coast of FB	Coast of FB
Joe_Bay_2E	P2	Mud_Creek_at_mouth	1.04	0.13	0.92	—	—	1341	0.846	-0.00	0.16	0.15	—	0.85	5.5	0.1	Coast of FB	Coast of FB
Joe_Bay_2E	P3	Stillwater_Creek	1.05	0.26	0.88	—	—	1359	0.779	-0.00	0.19	0.17	—	0.78	6.5	0.1	Coast of FB	Coast of FB
Joe_Bay_2E	P4	—	—	—	—	—	—	—	—	—	—	—	—	—	—	—	Coast of FB	—

Appendix 3. EDEN water-level estimation equations and performance statistics sorted by station name.—Continued

[n, number of data points; R^2, coefficient of determination; RMSE, root mean square error; WCA, Water Conservation Area; ENP, Everglades National Park; BCNP, Big Cypress National Preserve; FB, Florida Bay]

[a]Station name	[a]Predictor number	Predictor station name	Slope, m	y-intercept, b	Pearson correlation coefficient	[a]Minimum observed	[a]Maximum observed	n	R^2	Mean error	RMSE	Standard error	[a]Average measured, in feet	Nash-Sutcliffe	Percent model error	Percent model bias	Area of site	Area of predictor
L28_GAP	P1	BCA13	0.77	1.93	0.90	7.85	12.02	2783	0.786	−0.01	0.39	0.34	10.361	0.79	9.2	−0.1	BCNP	BCNP
L28_GAP	P2	BCA18	0.84	0.11	0.89	—	—	2224	0.798	−0.01	0.39	0.34	—	0.80	9.5	−0.0	BCNP	BCNP
L28_GAP	P3	BCA12	0.86	−0.37	0.88	—	—	2593	0.769	0.01	0.35	0.32	—	0.77	8.4	0.1	BCNP	BCNP
L28_GAP	P4	BCA4	0.67	5.27	0.85	—	—	2826	0.732	−0.01	0.44	0.37	—	0.73	10.5	−0.1	BCNP	BCNP
L28S1	P1	S140_H	0.84	1.77	0.93	7.14	10.10	1991	0.857	0.01	0.17	0.16	8.806	0.86	5.8	0.1	L28 Canal	L28 Canal
L28S1	P2	S140_H	0.84	1.77	0.93	—	—	1991	0.857	0.01	0.17	0.16	—	0.86	5.8	0.1	L28 Canal	L28 Canal
L28S1	P3	S140_H	0.84	1.77	0.93	—	—	1991	0.857	0.01	0.17	0.16	—	0.86	5.8	0.1	L28 Canal	L28 Canal
L28S1	P4	—	—	—	—	—	—	—	—	—	—	—	—	—	—	—	L28 Canal	—
L28S2	P1	3AN1W1	0.98	0.33	0.96	8.17	11.37	1903	0.855	−0.04	0.28	0.26	9.626	0.85	8.7	−0.4	L28 Canal	WCA 3A
L28S2	P2	W18	0.85	2.38	0.95	—	—	1565	0.845	−0.03	0.25	0.23	—	0.84	7.8	−0.3	L28 Canal	WCA 3A
L28S2	P3	EDEN_14	0.88	1.87	0.92	—	—	679	0.597	−0.08	0.29	0.25	—	0.59	9.2	−0.8	L28 Canal	WCA 3A
L28S2	P4	—	—	—	—	—	—	—	—	—	—	—	—	—	—	—	L28 Canal	—
L31N_1	P1	L31N_3	1.01	−0.05	1.00	3.68	7.74	3111	0.998	0.00	0.02	0.02	5.601	1.00	0.6	0.0	L31N Canal	L31N Canal
L31N_1	P2	L31N_4	1.00	−0.04	1.00	—	—	3125	0.998	0.00	0.03	0.03	—	1.00	0.7	0.0	L31N Canal	L31N Canal
L31N_1	P3	S335_T	1.01	1.86	1.00	—	—	3103	0.997	−0.00	0.03	0.03	—	1.00	0.8	−0.0	L31N Canal	L30 Canal
L31N_1	P4	—	—	—	—	—	—	—	—	—	—	—	—	—	—	—	L31N Canal	—
L31N_3	P1	L31N_1	0.99	0.06	1.00	3.65	7.73	3111	0.998	−0.00	0.02	0.02	5.594	1.00	0.6	−0.0	L31N Canal	L31N Canal
L31N_3	P2	L31N_4	0.99	0.01	1.00	—	—	3116	0.998	−0.00	0.03	0.03	—	1.00	0.6	−0.0	L31N Canal	L31N Canal
L31N_3	P3	S335_T	0.99	1.90	1.00	—	—	3094	0.995	−0.00	0.04	0.04	—	1.00	1.0	−0.0	L31N Canal	L30 Canal
L31N_3	P4	—	—	—	—	—	—	—	—	—	—	—	—	—	—	—	L31N Canal	—
L31N_4	P1	L31N_3	1.00	0.00	1.00	3.71	7.77	3116	0.998	0.00	0.03	0.03	5.625	1.00	0.6	0.0	L31N Canal	L31N Canal
L31N_4	P2	L31N_1	0.99	0.06	1.00	—	—	3125	0.998	−0.00	0.03	0.03	—	1.00	0.7	−0.0	L31N Canal	L31N Canal
L31N_4	P3	L31N_7	1.00	0.07	1.00	—	—	3115	0.996	−0.00	0.04	0.04	—	1.00	0.9	−0.0	L31N Canal	L31N Canal
L31N_4	P4	S335_T	1.00	1.91	1.00	—	—	3108	0.993	−0.00	0.05	0.05	—	0.99	1.2	−0.0	L31N Canal	L30 Canal

Appendix 3. EDEN water-level estimation equations and performance statistics sorted by station name.—Continued

[n, number of data points; R², coefficient of determination; RMSE, root mean square error; WCA, Water Conservation Area; ENP, Everglades National Park; BCNP, Big Cypress National Preserve; FB, Florida Bay]

[a]Station name	[a]Pre-dictor number	Predictor station name	Slope, m	y-intercept, b	Pearson correlation coefficient	[a]Minimum observed	[a]Maximum observed	n	R²	Mean error	RMSE	Standard error	[a]Average measured, in feet	Nash-Sutcliffe	Percent model error	Percent model bias	Area of site	Area of predictor
L31N_5	P1	S335_T	1.04	1.68	0.86	3.66	7.61	3064	0.991	0.02	0.07	0.06	5.565	0.99	1.7	0.4	L31N Canal	L30 Canal
L31N_5	P2	L31N_7	1.05	-0.30	0.84	—	—	3066	0.992	0.03	0.07	0.05	—	0.99	1.7	0.5	L31N Canal	L31N Canal
L31N_5	P3	L31N_4	1.04	-0.31	0.84	—	—	3081	0.997	0.03	0.05	0.03	—	0.99	1.3	0.5	L31N Canal	L31N Canal
L31N_5	P4	—	—	—	—	—	—	—	—	—	—	—	—	—	—	—	L31N Canal	—
L31N_7	P1	L31N_4	0.99	-0.04	1.00	3.65	7.65	3115	0.996	0.00	0.04	0.04	5.542	1.00	0.9	0.0	L31N Canal	L31N Canal
L31N_7	P2	L31N_1	0.99	0.01	1.00	—	—	3110	0.995	0.00	0.04	0.04	—	0.99	1.0	0.0	L31N Canal	L31N Canal
L31N_7	P3	L31N_3	1.00	-0.04	1.00	—	—	3101	0.995	0.00	0.04	0.04	—	0.99	1.0	0.0	L31N Canal	L31N Canal
L31N_7	P4	S344_T	0.61	0.74	0.75	—	—	2644	0.563	-0.00	0.38	0.29	—	0.56	9.5	-0.0	L31N Canal	BCNP
L31NN	P1	NESRS3	1.05	-0.55	1.00	2.33	6.16	1307	0.997	0.00	0.05	0.05	4.455	1.00	1.3	0.0	L31N Canal	ENP
L31NN	P2	S336_T	1.44	-0.91	0.96	—	—	1326	0.922	0.00	0.28	0.27	—	0.92	7.4	0.0	L31N Canal	Tamiami Canal
L31NN	P3	S334_T	1.58	-1.46	0.93	—	—	1322	0.859	0.00	0.38	0.35	—	0.86	9.9	0.0	L31N Canal	Tamiami Canal
L31NN	P4	—	—	—	—	—	—	—	—	—	—	—	—	—	—	—	L31N Canal	—
L31NS	P1	MET-1	2.05	-6.51	0.95	2.07	6.03	565	0.900	-0.00	0.33	0.31	3.993	0.92	8.3	-0.0	L31N Canal	ENP
L31NS	P2	S336_T	1.61	-2.18	0.94	—	—	1226	0.878	0.00	0.40	0.37	—	0.88	10.0	0.0	L31N Canal	Tamiami Canal
L31NS	P3	3BS1W1	1.16	-1.81	0.93	—	—	1210	0.868	0.00	0.41	0.39	—	0.87	10.5	0.0	L31N Canal	WCA 3B
L31NS	P4	—	—	—	—	—	—	—	—	—	—	—	—	—	—	—	L31N Canal	—
L31W	P1	S175_H	1.00	0.04	1.00	0.24	4.92	3021	0.998	0.00	0.04	0.04	2.747	1.00	1.0	0.0	ENP	L31W Canal
L31W	P2	NTS18	1.04	-0.19	0.99	—	—	2963	0.984	-0.00	0.14	0.14	—	0.98	3.0	-0.0	ENP	ENP
L31W	P3	NTS1	0.98	0.09	0.99	—	—	3011	0.972	0.00	0.18	0.18	—	0.97	3.9	0.0	ENP	ENP
L31W	P4	—	—	—	—	—	—	—	—	—	—	—	—	—	—	—	ENP	—
LOOP1_H	P1	LOOP1_T	1.03	-0.22	1.00	4.23	7.42	2646	0.997	-0.00	0.03	0.03	6.184	1.00	0.9	-0.0	BCNP	BCNP
LOOP1_H	P2	BCA9	0.67	2.49	0.94	—	—	2846	0.882	-0.00	0.17	0.16	—	0.88	5.5	-0.1	BCNP	BCNP
LOOP1_H	P3	LOOP2_H	0.66	2.80	0.93	—	—	2510	0.874	-0.01	0.18	0.17	—	0.87	5.7	-0.1	BCNP	BCNP
LOOP1_H	P4	S343B_T	1.00	-0.88	0.92	—	—	2703	0.810	-0.01	0.22	0.19	—	0.81	6.8	-0.2	BCNP	L28 Canal

Appendix 3. EDEN water-level estimation equations and performance statistics sorted by station name.—Continued

[n, number of data points; R², coefficient of determination; RMSE, root mean square error; WCA, Water Conservation Area; ENP, Everglades National Park; BCNP, Big Cypress National Preserve; FB, Florida Bay]

[a]Station name	[a]Predictor number	Predictor station name	Slope, m	y-intercept, b	Pearson correlation coefficient	[a]Minimum observed	[a]Maximum observed	n	R²	Mean error	RMSE	Standard error	[a]Average measured, in feet	Nash-Sutcliffe	Percent model error	Percent model bias	Area of site	Area of predictor
LOOP1_T	P1	LOOP1_H	0.96	0.24	1.00	3.15	7.34	2646	0.997	0.00	0.03	0.03	6.158	1.00	0.7	0.0	BCNP	BCNP
LOOP1_T	P2	LOOP2_H	0.66	2.79	0.95	—	—	2497	0.892	-0.01	0.20	0.18	—	0.89	4.7	-0.2	BCNP	BCNP
LOOP1_T	P3	BCA9	0.66	2.58	0.94	—	—	2767	0.880	-0.01	0.19	0.17	—	0.88	4.4	-0.1	BCNP	BCNP
LOOP1_T	P4	S343B_T	1.07	-1.34	0.91	—	—	2644	0.776	-0.02	0.28	0.23	—	0.77	6.6	-0.3	BCNP	L28 Canal
LOOP2_H	P1	LOOP2_T	1.13	-0.56	0.98	1.41	6.61	2544	0.967	0.00	0.14	0.14	5.075	0.97	2.6	0.1	BCNP	BCNP
LOOP2_H	P2	LOOP1_T	1.35	-3.24	0.95	—	—	2497	0.892	0.01	0.27	0.27	—	0.89	5.3	0.2	BCNP	BCNP
LOOP2_H	P3	BCA9	1.00	-0.39	0.94	—	—	2735	0.887	0.00	0.27	0.25	—	0.89	5.1	0.1	BCNP	BCNP
LOOP2_H	P4	BCA10	0.82	3.06	0.92	—	—	2722	0.853	-0.01	0.30	0.27	—	0.85	5.8	-0.1	BCNP	BCNP
LOOP2_T	P1	LOOP2_H	0.85	0.66	0.98	2.17	6.06	2544	0.967	-0.00	0.12	0.12	4.994	0.97	3.1	-0.1	BCNP	BCNP
LOOP2_T	P2	BCA10	0.70	3.27	0.93	—	—	2737	0.859	-0.01	0.24	0.22	—	0.86	6.3	-0.2	BCNP	BCNP
LOOP2_T	P3	BCA6	0.62	1.18	0.92	—	—	1027	0.726	-0.05	0.38	0.30	—	0.72	9.7	-1.0	BCNP	BCNP
LOOP2_T	P4	—	—	—	—	—	—	—	—	—	—	—	—	—	—	—	BCNP	—
McCormick_Creek_at_mouth	P1	Mud_Creek_at_mouth	1.01	0.06	0.96	-1.46	2.11	3050	0.931	-0.00	0.10	0.10	-0.547	0.93	2.8	0.0	Coast of FB	Coast of FB
McCormick_Creek_at_mouth	P2	Taylor_River_at_mouth	1.02	0.08	0.95	—	—	3128	0.908	0.00	0.11	0.11	—	0.91	3.2	-0.0	Coast of FB	Coast of FB
McCormick_Creek_at_mouth	P3	Trout_Creek_at_mouth	0.99	0.04	0.97	—	—	3110	0.946	-0.00	0.09	0.09	—	0.95	2.5	0.0	Coast of FB	Coast of FB
McCormick_Creek_at_mouth	P4	—	—	—	—	—	—	—	—	—	—	—	—	—	—	—	Coast of FB	—
MET-1	P1	NE2	0.72	0.45	0.98	4.12	5.81	641	0.956	-0.00	0.10	0.09	4.964	0.96	5.7	-0.0	ENP	ENP
MET-1	P2	NE1	1.15	-2.62	0.97	—	—	693	0.946	-0.00	0.11	0.11	—	0.95	6.6	-0.0	ENP	ENP
MET-1	P3	3BS1W1	0.63	2.03	0.96	—	—	638	0.922	-0.00	0.14	0.13	—	0.92	8.3	-0.0	ENP	WCA 3B
MET-1	P4	—	—	—	—	—	—	—	—	—	—	—	—	—	—	—	ENP	—

Appendix 3.   EDEN water-level estimation equations and performance statistics sorted by station name.—Continued

[n, number of data points; R², coefficient of determination; RMSE, root mean square error; WCA, Water Conservation Area; ENP, Everglades National Park; BCNP, Big Cypress National Preserve; FB, Florida Bay]

[a]Station name	[a]Predictor number	Predictor station name	Slope, m	y-intercept, b	Pearson correlation coefficient	[a]Minimum observed	[a]Maximum observed	n	R²	Mean error	RMSE	Standard error	[a]Average measured, in feet	Nash-Sutcliffe	Percent model error	Percent model bias	Area of site	Area of predictor
Mud_Creek_at_mouth	P1	Taylor_River_at_mouth	1.02	0.02	0.99	-1.65	2.00	3075	0.979	0.00	0.05	0.05	-0.603	0.98	1.4	-0.0	Coast of FB	Coast of FB
Mud_Creek_at_mouth	P2	Trout_Creek_at_mouth	0.97	-0.03	0.99	—	—	3057	0.976	-0.00	0.06	0.05	—	0.98	1.5	0.0	Coast of FB	Coast of FB
Mud_Creek_at_mouth	P3	McCormick_Creek_at_mouth	0.92	-0.09	0.96	—	—	3050	0.931	0.00	0.10	0.09	—	0.93	2.6	-0.0	Coast of FB	Coast of FB
Mud_Creek_at_mouth	P4	—	—	—	—	—	—	—	—	—	—	—	—	—	—	—	Coast of FB	—
NCL	P1	CP	1.03	0.07	0.99	-2.79	1.48	3014	0.978	-0.00	0.09	0.09	-0.281	0.98	2.1	0.4	ENP	ENP
NCL	P2	Taylor_Slough_wetland_at_E146	1.07	0.11	0.97	—	—	968	0.953	-0.01	0.09	0.08	—	0.98	2.0	1.8	ENP	ENP
NCL	P3	E146	1.18	0.22	0.97	—	—	3044	0.942	-0.01	0.15	0.14	—	0.94	3.5	2.2	ENP	ENP
NCL	P4	—	—	—	—	—	—	—	—	—	—	—	—	—	—	—	ENP	—
NE1	P1	NE5	0.83	1.39	0.97	4.76	8.01	3080	0.948	0.00	0.11	0.10	6.875	0.95	3.2	0.0	ENP	ENP
NE1	P2	MET-1	0.82	2.51	0.97	—	—	693	0.946	0.00	0.09	0.09	—	0.96	2.9	0.0	ENP	ENP
NE1	P3	NE4	0.77	1.74	0.96	—	—	2888	0.931	0.00	0.13	0.12	—	0.93	3.9	0.0	ENP	ENP
NE1	P4	—	—	—	—	—	—	—	—	—	—	—	—	—	—	—	ENP	—
NE2	P1	MET-1	1.33	-0.31	0.98	4.51	7.98	641	0.956	0.00	0.13	0.13	6.723	0.97	3.8	0.0	ENP	ENP
NE2	P2	NE1	1.19	-1.51	0.95	—	—	2909	0.896	0.00	0.18	0.17	—	0.90	5.2	0.0	ENP	ENP
NE2	P3	NE4	0.97	0.29	0.93	—	—	2790	0.870	0.00	0.21	0.19	—	0.87	6.0	0.0	ENP	ENP
NE2	P4	—	—	—	—	—	—	—	—	—	—	—	—	—	—	—	ENP	—
NE4	P1	NE5	1.06	-0.36	0.99	4.50	7.84	2904	0.983	0.00	0.08	0.07	6.622	0.98	2.3	0.0	ENP	ENP
NE4	P2	NE1	1.20	-1.64	0.96	—	—	2888	0.931	-0.00	0.16	0.15	—	0.93	4.7	-0.0	ENP	ENP
NE4	P3	NE2	0.90	0.61	0.93	—	—	2790	0.870	-0.00	0.20	0.19	—	0.87	6.0	-0.0	ENP	ENP
NE4	P4	—	—	—	—	—	—	—	—	—	—	—	—	—	—	—	ENP	—
NE5	P1	NE4	0.93	0.44	0.99	5.08	7.78	2904	0.983	-0.00	0.07	0.07	6.606	0.98	2.6	-0.0	ENP	ENP
NE5	P2	NE1	1.14	-1.23	0.97	—	—	3080	0.948	-0.00	0.12	0.12	—	0.95	4.6	-0.0	ENP	ENP
NE5	P3	MET-1	1.04	1.04	0.96	—	—	719	0.918	-0.00	0.15	0.14	—	0.95	5.5	-0.0	ENP	ENP
NE5	P4	—	—	—	—	—	—	—	—	—	—	—	—	—	—	—	ENP	—

Appendix 3. EDEN water-level estimation equations and performance statistics sorted by station name.—Continued

[n, number of data points; R², coefficient of determination; RMSE, root mean square error; WCA, Water Conservation Area; ENP, Everglades National Park; BCNP, Big Cypress National Preserve; FB, Florida Bay]

[a]Station name	[a]Predictor number	Predictor station name	Slope, m	y-intercept, b	Pearson correlation coefficient	[a]Minimum observed	[a]Maximum observed	n	R²	Mean error	RMSE	Standard error	[a]Average measured, in feet	Nash-Sutcliffe	Percent model error	Percent model bias	Area of site	Area of predictor
NESRS3	P1	L31NN	0.95	0.54	1.00	3.04	6.66	1307	0.997	0.00	0.05	0.05	5.100	1.00	1.3	0.0	ENP	L31N Canal
NESRS3	P2	S336_T	1.31	-0.06	0.93	—	—	2821	0.873	0.00	0.32	0.30	—	0.87	9.0	0.1	ENP	Tamiami Canal
NESRS3	P3	NE2	1.46	-4.65	0.92	—	—	2716	0.844	0.00	0.34	0.32	—	0.84	9.5	0.1	ENP	ENP
NESRS3	P4	—	—	—	—	—	—	—	—	—	—	—	—	—	—	—	ENP	—
NORTH_CA1	P1	SOUTH_CA1	0.85	2.81	0.91	14.02	17.90	2555	0.826	0.00	0.38	0.35	15.789	0.83	9.8	0.0	WCA1	WCA1
NORTH_CA1	P2	EDEN_13	0.43	11.71	0.81	—	—	745	0.652	-0.00	0.19	0.16	—	0.93	5.0	-0.0	WCA1	WCA2B
NORTH_CA1	P3	EDEN_8	0.46	11.44	0.74	—	—	806	0.548	0.00	0.24	0.18	—	0.91	6.3	0.0	WCA1	WCA3A
NORTH_CA1	P4	—	—	—	—	—	—	—	—	—	—	—	—	—	—	—	WCA1	—
NP201	P1	NP202	1.25	-0.85	0.95	2.90	7.65	3135	0.895	-0.00	0.27	0.25	5.896	0.90	5.6	-0.0	ENP	ENP
NP201	P2	NP203	1.25	0.09	0.94	—	—	3106	0.876	0.00	0.29	0.27	—	0.88	6.1	0.1	ENP	ENP
NP201	P3	P33	1.50	-1.29	0.91	—	—	3136	0.836	-0.00	0.33	0.30	—	0.84	7.0	-0.0	ENP	ENP
NP201	P4	—	—	—	—	—	—	—	—	—	—	—	—	—	—	—	ENP	—
NP202	P1	NP203	0.99	0.84	0.97	3.66	6.87	3116	0.950	0.00	0.14	0.14	5.413	0.95	4.4	0.0	ENP	ENP
NP202	P2	P33	1.20	-0.34	0.97	—	—	3146	0.931	0.00	0.16	0.16	—	0.93	5.1	0.0	ENP	ENP
NP202	P3	NP201	0.72	1.18	0.95	—	—	3135	0.895	0.00	0.20	0.19	—	0.90	6.3	0.0	ENP	ENP
NP202	P4	—	—	—	—	—	—	—	—	—	—	—	—	—	—	—	ENP	—
NP203	P1	P33	1.21	-1.18	0.98	2.64	5.99	3117	0.968	0.00	0.11	0.11	4.639	0.97	3.3	0.0	ENP	ENP
NP203	P2	NP202	0.96	-0.57	0.97	—	—	3116	0.950	-0.00	0.14	0.14	—	0.95	4.2	-0.0	ENP	ENP
NP203	P3	NE5	1.05	-2.30	0.93	—	—	3079	0.859	0.01	0.22	0.21	—	0.86	6.7	0.1	ENP	ENP
NP203	P4	—	—	—	—	—	—	—	—	—	—	—	—	—	—	—	ENP	—
NP205	P1	LOOP2_H	1.06	-0.77	0.92	1.06	6.29	2769	0.841	-0.02	0.39	0.36	4.583	0.84	7.5	-0.5	ENP	BCNP
NP205	P2	BCA9	1.12	-1.48	0.90	—	—	3113	0.809	-0.02	0.41	0.36	—	0.81	7.8	-0.4	ENP	BCNP
NP205	P3	P34	1.14	3.21	0.87	—	—	3114	0.766	-0.00	0.47	0.41	—	0.77	8.9	-0.0	ENP	ENP
NP205	P4	—	—	—	—	—	—	—	—	—	—	—	—	—	—	—	ENP	—
NP206	P1	CR3	0.91	0.81	0.98	0.67	5.73	3155	0.958	-0.00	0.21	0.20	4.004	0.96	4.1	-0.0	ENP	ENP
NP206	P2	RG1	0.96	0.19	0.98	—	—	3127	0.952	-0.00	0.22	0.22	—	0.95	4.4	-0.0	ENP	ENP
NP206	P3	RG2	0.91	0.67	0.97	—	—	3128	0.944	-0.00	0.24	0.23	—	0.94	4.8	-0.1	ENP	ENP
NP206	P4	—	—	—	—	—	—	—	—	—	—	—	—	—	—	—	ENP	—
NP44	P1	DO2	1.29	0.29	0.98	-1.70	4.34	3153	0.963	0.00	0.25	0.24	1.869	0.96	4.1	0.2	ENP	ENP
NP44	P2	DO1	1.31	0.58	0.97	—	—	3153	0.954	0.00	0.28	0.27	—	0.95	4.6	0.2	ENP	ENP
NP44	P3	NP72	1.07	0.41	0.97	—	—	3129	0.950	0.00	0.29	0.28	—	0.95	4.7	0.1	ENP	ENP
NP44	P4	—	—	—	—	—	—	—	—	—	—	—	—	—	—	—	ENP	—

Appendix 3. EDEN water-level estimation equations and performance statistics sorted by station name.—Continued

[n, number of data points; R², coefficient of determination; RMSE, root mean square error; WCA, Water Conservation Area; ENP, Everglades National Park; BCNP, Big Cypress National Preserve; FB, Florida Bay]

[a]Station name	[a]Predictor number	Predictor station name	Slope, m	y-intercept, b	Pearson correlation coefficient	[a]Minimum observed	[a]Maximum observed	n	R²	Mean error	RMSE	Standard error	[a]Average measured, in feet	Nash-Sutcliffe	Percent model error	Percent model bias	Area of site	Area of predictor
NP46	P1	CY3	0.82	-0.50	0.95	-2.31	1.69	3143	0.946	0.01	0.16	0.15	-0.097	0.95	3.9	-8.8	ENP	ENP
NP46	P2	SP	0.83	-0.56	0.94	—	—	3084	0.903	0.01	0.21	0.20	—	0.90	5.3	-8.3	ENP	ENP
NP46	P3	DO2	0.64	-0.89	0.93	—	—	3143	0.897	0.01	0.22	0.20	—	0.90	5.4	-8.8	ENP	ENP
NP46	P4	—	—	—	—	—	—	—	—	—	—	—	—	—	—	—	ENP	—
NP62	P1	A13	0.77	-1.09	0.94	-1.70	2.74	3139	0.889	0.00	0.26	0.25	1.127	0.89	5.9	0.0	ENP	ENP
NP62	P2	SP	0.95	0.61	0.93	—	—	3080	0.860	0.00	0.29	0.27	—	0.86	6.6	0.0	ENP	ENP
NP62	P3	P38	1.31	1.02	0.92	—	—	3052	0.722	-0.05	0.43	0.41	—	0.70	9.7	-4.1	ENP	ENP
NP62	P4	—	—	—	—	—	—	—	—	—	—	—	—	—	—	—	ENP	—
NP67	P1	TSH	1.09	0.13	0.96	-1.75	2.07	3116	0.942	0.00	0.16	0.15	0.540	0.94	4.2	0.7	ENP	ENP
NP67	P2	R127	0.93	-0.06	0.95	—	—	3099	0.934	0.01	0.17	0.16	—	0.93	4.5	1.2	ENP	ENP
NP67	P3	TSB	0.56	-0.47	0.94	—	—	1799	0.889	-0.00	0.23	0.21	—	0.89	5.9	-0.0	ENP	ENP
NP67	P4	—	—	—	—	—	—	—	—	—	—	—	—	—	—	—	ENP	—
NP72	P1	DO1	1.20	0.19	0.98	-1.74	3.65	3131	0.960	0.00	0.23	0.23	1.370	0.96	4.3	0.1	ENP	ENP
NP72	P2	DO2	1.17	-0.07	0.98	—	—	3131	0.955	0.00	0.25	0.24	—	0.95	4.6	0.1	ENP	ENP
NP72	P3	NP44	0.88	-0.29	0.97	—	—	3129	0.950	-0.00	0.26	0.25	—	0.95	4.9	-0.1	ENP	ENP
NP72	P4	—	—	—	—	—	—	—	—	—	—	—	—	—	—	—	ENP	—
NTS1	P1	L31W	1.00	-0.01	0.99	0.22	6.68	3011	0.972	-0.00	0.19	0.18	2.731	0.97	2.9	-0.0	ENP	ENP
NTS1	P2	S175_H	0.99	0.03	0.99	—	—	3113	0.970	-0.00	0.19	0.19	—	0.97	2.9	-0.0	ENP	L31W Canal
NTS1	P3	E112	0.98	0.29	0.98	—	—	3129	0.968	0.00	0.20	0.19	—	0.97	3.0	0.0	ENP	ENP
NTS1	P4	—	—	—	—	—	—	—	—	—	—	—	—	—	—	—	ENP	—
NTS10	P1	E112	1.03	0.44	0.98	0.18	5.03	3154	0.968	-0.00	0.21	0.20	2.995	0.97	4.3	-0.0	ENP	ENP
NTS10	P2	R3110	0.93	0.32	0.98	—	—	3154	0.961	0.00	0.23	0.22	—	0.96	4.7	0.0	ENP	ENP
NTS10	P3	NTS1	1.03	0.19	0.98	—	—	3128	0.960	0.00	0.23	0.23	—	0.96	4.7	0.0	ENP	ENP
NTS10	P4	—	—	—	—	—	—	—	—	—	—	—	—	—	—	—	ENP	—
NTS14	P1	NP72	1.13	0.58	0.97	-1.08	4.84	3083	0.942	-0.00	0.32	0.31	2.148	0.94	5.4	-0.1	ENP	ENP
NTS14	P2	DO1	1.39	0.76	0.97	—	—	3107	0.939	0.00	0.33	0.32	—	0.94	5.6	0.0	ENP	ENP
NTS14	P3	NP44	1.02	0.22	0.96	—	—	3105	0.930	-0.00	0.35	0.34	—	0.93	6.0	-0.1	ENP	ENP
NTS14	P4	—	—	—	—	—	—	—	—	—	—	—	—	—	—	—	ENP	—
NTS18	P1	L31W	0.94	0.22	0.99	0.39	5.26	2963	0.984	0.00	0.13	0.13	2.789	0.98	2.7	0.0	ENP	ENP
NTS18	P2	S175_H	0.94	0.26	0.99	—	—	3065	0.981	0.00	0.14	0.14	—	0.98	2.9	0.0	ENP	L31W Canal
NTS18	P3	NTS10	0.87	0.20	0.98	—	—	3080	0.957	0.00	0.21	0.21	—	0.96	4.4	0.0	ENP	ENP
NTS18	P4	—	—	—	—	—	—	—	—	—	—	—	—	—	—	—	ENP	—

Appendix 3. EDEN water-level estimation equations and performance statistics sorted by station name.—Continued

[n, number of data points; R^2, coefficient of determination; RMSE, root mean square error; WCA, Water Conservation Area; ENP, Everglades National Park; BCNP, Big Cypress National Preserve; FB, Florida Bay]

Station name	Predictor number	Predictor station name	Slope, m	y-intercept, b	Pearson correlation coefficient	Minimum observed	Maximum observed	n	R^2	Mean error	RMSE	Standard error	Average measured, in feet	Nash-Sutcliffe	Percent model error	Percent model bias	Area of site	Area of predictor
NWWF	P1	L31NS	0.79	1.40	0.83	2.78	6.43	1222	0.690	0.00	0.60	0.50	4.411	0.70	16.5	0.0	Pennsuco Wetlands	L31N Canal
NWWF	P2	CT50R	1.74	3.92	0.83	—	—	1990	0.686	0.00	0.57	0.47	—	0.69	15.6	0.0	Pennsuco Wetlands	ENP
NWWF	P3	S337_T	1.19	-0.92	0.77	—	—	1868	0.598	0.00	0.65	0.50	—	0.60	17.8	0.0	Pennsuco Wetlands	L30 Canal
NWWF	P4	—	—	—	—	—	—	—	—	—	—	—	—	—	—	—	Pennsuco Wetlands	—
OL	P1	Taylor Slough wetland at E146	0.92	0.02	0.93	-2.40	1.67	1030	0.873	0.00	0.12	0.12	-0.277	0.92	3.0	-0.1	ENP	ENP
OL	P2	E146	0.92	0.12	0.89	—	—	3121	0.867	-0.00	0.19	0.17	—	0.87	4.6	1.6	ENP	ENP
OL	P3	TSH	0.82	-0.58	0.89	—	—	3155	0.869	-0.00	0.19	0.18	—	0.87	4.8	1.6	ENP	ENP
OL	P4	—	—	—	—	—	—	—	—	—	—	—	—	—	—	—	ENP	—
OT	P1	P34	0.83	-0.44	0.95	-1.29	2.01	3029	0.906	0.00	0.20	0.19	0.550	0.91	6.0	0.2	ENP	ENP
OT	P2	EDEN_3	1.38	0.20	0.95	—	—	899	0.893	0.00	0.17	0.17	—	0.89	5.3	0.3	ENP	ENP
OT	P3	P36	1.12	-2.48	0.89	—	—	3066	0.794	-0.00	0.29	0.26	—	0.79	8.8	-0.1	ENP	ENP
OT	P4	—	—	—	—	—	—	—	—	—	—	—	—	—	—	—	ENP	—
P33	P1	NP203	0.80	1.10	0.98	3.26	6.07	3117	0.968	-0.00	0.09	0.09	4.799	0.97	3.2	-0.0	ENP	ENP
P33	P2	NP202	0.78	0.59	0.97	—	—	3146	0.931	-0.00	0.13	0.13	—	0.93	4.7	-0.0	ENP	ENP
P33	P3	NE5	0.86	-0.84	0.95	—	—	3109	0.895	-0.00	0.16	0.15	—	0.90	5.6	-0.0	ENP	ENP
P33	P4	—	—	—	—	—	—	—	—	—	—	—	—	—	—	—	ENP	—
P34	P1	OT	1.09	0.59	0.95	-1.43	3.11	3029	0.906	-0.00	0.23	0.21	1.201	0.91	5.0	-0.2	ENP	ENP
P34	P2	P36	1.32	-2.38	0.91	—	—	3118	0.834	-0.00	0.30	0.28	—	0.83	6.6	-0.0	ENP	ENP
P34	P3	EDEN_3	1.31	0.87	0.90	—	—	959	0.813	0.00	0.24	0.22	—	0.81	5.4	0.0	ENP	ENP
P34	P4	—	—	—	—	—	—	—	—	—	—	—	—	—	—	—	ENP	—
P35	P1	OT	0.73	-0.19	0.86	-1.18	1.88	3060	0.732	0.00	0.28	0.24	0.220	0.73	9.2	0.9	ENP	ENP
P35	P2	P38	0.81	0.15	0.83	—	—	3062	0.541	-0.03	0.38	0.33	—	0.51	12.3	-12.8	ENP	ENP
P35	P3	P34	0.59	-0.50	0.81	—	—	3112	0.660	0.00	0.32	0.26	—	0.66	10.3	0.1	ENP	ENP
P35	P4	—	—	—	—	—	—	—	—	—	—	—	—	—	—	—	ENP	—
P36	P1	NP203	0.81	-1.02	0.97	1.03	4.01	3121	0.940	0.00	0.13	0.12	2.721	0.94	4.2	0.1	ENP	ENP
P36	P2	P33	0.98	-1.98	0.96	—	—	3151	0.924	0.00	0.14	0.14	—	0.92	4.7	0.0	ENP	ENP
P36	P3	NP202	0.77	-1.43	0.94	—	—	3150	0.876	0.00	0.18	0.17	—	0.88	6.1	0.0	ENP	ENP
P36	P4	—	—	—	—	—	—	—	—	—	—	—	—	—	—	—	ENP	—

Appendix 3. EDEN water-level estimation equations and performance statistics sorted by station name.—Continued

[n, number of data points; R², coefficient of determination; RMSE, root mean square error; WCA, Water Conservation Area; ENP, Everglades National Park; BCNP, Big Cypress National Preserve; FB, Florida Bay]

Station name	Predictor number	Predictor station name	Slope, m	y-intercept, b	Pearson correlation coefficient	Minimum observed	Maximum observed	n	R²	Mean error	RMSE	Standard error	Average measured, in feet	Nash-Sutcliffe	Percent model error	Percent model bias	Area of site	Area of predictor
P37	P1	Taylor_Slough_wetland_at_E146	1.01	0.23	0.98	-2.44	1.55	1030	0.961	-0.00	0.07	0.07	-0.125	0.98	1.8	0.2	ENP	ENP
P37	P2	TSH	1.00	-0.50	0.97	—	—	3155	0.946	0.00	0.14	0.14	—	0.95	3.5	-0.0	ENP	ENP
P37	P3	E146	1.07	0.33	0.97	—	—	3121	0.935	-0.00	0.14	0.14	—	0.94	3.6	0.0	ENP	ENP
P37	P4	—	—	—	—	—	—	—	—	—	—	—	—	—	—	—	ENP	—
P38	P1	NP62	0.65	-0.65	0.92	-1.87	1.92	3052	0.722	0.04	0.32	0.27	0.110	0.72	8.3	31.9	ENP	ENP
P38	P2	SP	0.66	-0.28	0.92	—	—	3009	0.701	0.04	0.33	0.28	—	0.70	8.7	32.3	ENP	ENP
P38	P3	NP46	0.72	0.15	0.89	—	—	3056	0.717	0.03	0.32	0.26	—	0.71	8.4	26.1	ENP	ENP
P38	P4	—	—	—	—	—	—	—	—	—	—	—	—	—	—	—	ENP	—
R127	P1	TSH	1.13	0.23	0.98	-1.62	2.30	3138	0.975	-0.00	0.11	0.11	0.645	0.97	2.8	-0.4	ENP	ENP
R127	P2	S175_T	1.17	-0.45	0.97	—	—	3108	0.950	-0.00	0.15	0.15	—	0.95	3.9	-0.4	ENP	L31W Canal
R127	P3	TSB	0.60	-0.45	0.97	—	—	1799	0.932	-0.00	0.19	0.18	—	0.93	4.8	-0.0	ENP	ENP
R127	P4	—	—	—	—	—	—	—	—	—	—	—	—	—	—	—	ENP	—
R3110	P1	NTS10	1.03	-0.22	0.98	-0.43	5.01	3154	0.961	-0.00	0.24	0.23	2.869	0.96	4.4	-0.0	ENP	ENP
R3110	P2	E112	1.07	0.21	0.97	—	—	3155	0.949	-0.00	0.28	0.27	—	0.95	5.0	-0.0	ENP	ENP
R3110	P3	CR2	1.04	-0.84	0.97	—	—	3118	0.941	-0.00	0.29	0.29	—	0.94	5.4	-0.0	ENP	ENP
R3110	P4	—	—	—	—	—	—	—	—	—	—	—	—	—	—	—	ENP	—
RG1	P1	RG2	0.94	0.54	0.98	0.78	5.87	3100	0.966	-0.00	0.19	0.19	3.974	0.97	3.7	-0.0	ENP	ENP
RG1	P2	NP206	0.99	0.00	0.98	—	—	3127	0.952	0.00	0.23	0.22	—	0.95	4.5	0.0	ENP	ENP
RG1	P3	CR2	0.88	0.84	0.96	—	—	3090	0.925	-0.00	0.29	0.27	—	0.92	5.6	-0.0	ENP	ENP
RG1	P4	—	—	—	—	—	—	—	—	—	—	—	—	—	—	—	ENP	—
RG2	P1	CR2	0.94	0.31	0.98	-0.20	5.64	3091	0.969	0.00	0.19	0.19	3.648	0.97	3.3	0.0	ENP	ENP
RG2	P2	RG1	1.03	-0.43	0.98	—	—	3100	0.966	0.00	0.20	0.20	—	0.97	3.4	0.0	ENP	ENP
RG2	P3	NP206	1.03	-0.49	0.97	—	—	3128	0.944	0.00	0.26	0.25	—	0.94	4.4	0.1	ENP	ENP
RG2	P4	—	—	—	—	—	—	—	—	—	—	—	—	—	—	—	ENP	—
S10A_H	P1	S10C_H	1.00	-0.05	1.00	12.06	17.46	3081	0.998	-0.00	0.04	0.04	15.978	1.00	0.7	-0.0	L39 Canal	L39 Canal
S10A_H	P2	S10D_H	1.01	-0.19	1.00	—	—	3073	0.994	-0.00	0.06	0.06	—	0.99	1.2	-0.0	L39 Canal	L39 Canal
S10A_H	P3	S39_H	0.96	2.25	0.99	—	—	2560	0.976	-0.00	0.14	0.14	—	0.98	2.6	-0.0	L39 Canal	L39 Canal
S10A_H	P4	—	—	—	—	—	—	—	—	—	—	—	—	—	—	—	L39 Canal	—
S10A_T	P1	S10C_T	0.96	0.49	1.00	11.44	16.14	2945	0.995	-0.00	0.06	0.06	12.887	0.99	1.3	-0.0	WCA 2A	WCA 2A
S10A_T	P2	S10D_T	0.92	0.93	0.99	—	—	2964	0.989	0.00	0.09	0.08	—	0.99	1.8	0.0	WCA 2A	WCA 2A
S10A_T	P3	SITE_19	0.74	3.91	0.80	—	—	2926	0.639	0.00	0.49	0.39	—	0.64	10.5	0.0	WCA 2A	WCA 2A
S10A_T	P4	—	—	—	—	—	—	—	—	—	—	—	—	—	—	—	—	WCA 2A

Appendix 3. EDEN water-level estimation equations and performance statistics sorted by station name.—Continued

[n, number of data points; R², coefficient of determination; RMSE, root mean square error; WCA, Water Conservation Area; ENP, Everglades National Park; BCNP, Big Cypress National Preserve; FB, Florida Bay]

[a]Station name	[a]Predictor number	Predictor station name	Slope, m	y-intercept, b	Pearson correlation coefficient	[a]Minimum observed	[a]Maximum observed	n	R²	Mean error	RMSE	Standard error	[a]Average measured, in feet	Nash-Sutcliffe	Percent model error	Percent model bias	Area of site	Area of predictor
S10C_H	P1	S10A_H	1.00	0.08	1.00	11.88	17.49	3081	0.998	0.00	0.04	0.04	16.007	1.00	0.7	0.0	L39 Canal	L39 Canal
S10C_H	P2	S10D_H	1.01	-0.10	1.00	—	—	3112	0.996	0.00	0.05	0.05	—	1.00	0.9	0.0	L39 Canal	L39 Canal
S10C_H	P3	S39_H	0.96	2.30	0.99	—	—	2596	0.980	-0.00	0.13	0.12	—	0.98	2.2	-0.0	L39 Canal	L39 Canal
S10C_H	P4	—	—	—	—	—	—	—	—	—	—	—	—	—	—	—	L39 Canal	—
S10C_T	P1	S10D_T	0.96	0.45	1.00	11.46	16.20	2967	0.995	0.00	0.06	0.06	12.918	1.00	1.3	0.0	WCA 2A	WCA 2A
S10C_T	P2	S10A_T	1.04	-0.44	1.00	—	—	2945	0.995	0.00	0.06	0.06	—	0.99	1.3	0.0	WCA 2A	WCA 2A
S10C_T	P3	SITE_19	0.76	3.70	0.79	—	—	2928	0.619	0.00	0.53	0.41	—	0.62	11.1	0.0	WCA 2A	WCA 2A
S10C_T	P4	—	—	—	—	—	—	—	—	—	—	—	—	—	—	—	WCA 2A	—
S10D_H	P1	S10C_H	0.99	0.16	1.00	13.33	17.48	3112	0.996	-0.00	0.05	0.05	16.043	1.00	1.2	-0.0	L39 Canal	L39 Canal
S10D_H	P2	S10A_H	0.98	0.28	1.00	—	—	3073	0.994	0.00	0.06	0.06	—	0.99	1.5	0.0	L39 Canal	L39 Canal
S10D_H	P3	S39_H	0.96	2.36	0.99	—	—	2586	0.975	-0.00	0.13	0.13	—	0.97	3.2	-0.0	L39 Canal	L39 Canal
S10D_H	P4	—	—	—	—	—	—	—	—	—	—	—	—	—	—	—	L39 Canal	—
S10D_T	P1	S10C_T	1.03	-0.40	1.00	11.46	16.28	2967	0.995	-0.00	0.06	0.06	12.944	1.00	1.3	-0.0	WCA 2A	WCA 2A
S10D_T	P2	S10A_T	1.07	-0.86	0.99	—	—	2964	0.989	-0.00	0.09	0.09	—	0.99	1.9	-0.0	WCA 2A	WCA 2A
S10D_T	P3	EDEN_11	1.30	-1.84	0.81	—	—	739	0.649	0.00	0.51	0.41	—	0.65	10.6	0.0	WCA 2A	WCA 2A
S10D_T	P4	—	—	—	—	—	—	—	—	—	—	—	—	—	—	—	WCA 2A	—
S11A_H	P1	S11B_H	1.00	0.00	1.00	9.66	14.27	3052	1.000	-0.00	0.02	0.02	11.823	1.00	0.4	-0.0	WCA 2A	WCA 2A
S11A_H	P2	S11C_H	1.00	0.03	1.00	—	—	3038	0.999	-0.00	0.04	0.04	—	1.00	0.8	-0.0	WCA 2A	WCA 2A
S11A_H	P3	S144_H	0.96	2.12	0.99	—	—	2834	0.974	-0.00	0.16	0.15	—	0.97	3.4	-0.0	WCA 2A	WCA 2A
S11A_H	P4	—	—	—	—	—	—	—	—	—	—	—	—	—	—	—	WCA 2A	—
S11A_T	P1	S11B_T	0.98	0.13	1.00	7.54	12.87	2936	0.998	-0.00	0.05	0.05	9.967	1.00	0.9	-0.0	WCA 3A	WCA 3A
S11A_T	P2	S142_H	1.00	1.50	1.00	—	—	2881	0.997	0.00	0.06	0.06	—	1.00	1.2	0.0	WCA 3A	L38E Canal
S11A_T	P3	S11C_T	0.97	0.20	1.00	—	—	2980	0.996	-0.00	0.07	0.07	—	1.00	1.4	-0.0	WCA 3A	WCA 3A
S11A_T	P4	—	—	—	—	—	—	—	—	—	—	—	—	—	—	—	WCA 3A	—
S11B_H	P1	S11A_H	1.00	0.00	1.00	9.69	14.28	3052	1.000	0.00	0.02	0.02	11.832	1.00	0.4	0.0	WCA 2A	WCA 2A
S11B_H	P2	S11C_H	1.00	0.04	1.00	—	—	3092	0.999	0.00	0.03	0.03	—	1.00	0.6	-0.0	WCA 2A	WCA 2A
S11B_H	P3	S144_H	0.96	2.15	0.99	—	—	2867	0.971	-0.00	0.16	0.16	—	0.97	3.6	-0.0	WCA 2A	WCA 2A
S11B_H	P4	—	—	—	—	—	—	—	—	—	—	—	—	—	—	—	WCA 2A	—
S11B_T	P1	S11C_T	0.99	0.11	1.00	8.01	12.99	2941	0.999	-0.00	0.04	0.04	10.103	1.00	0.8	-0.0	WCA 3A	WCA 3A
S11B_T	P2	S11A_T	1.01	-0.11	1.00	—	—	2936	0.998	0.00	0.05	0.05	—	1.00	1.0	0.0	WCA 3A	WCA 3A
S11B_T	P3	S142_H	1.02	1.41	1.00	—	—	2749	0.995	0.00	0.07	0.07	—	1.00	1.5	0.0	WCA 3A	L38E Canal
S11B_T	P4	—	—	—	—	—	—	—	—	—	—	—	—	—	—	—	WCA 3A	—
S11C_H	P1	S11B_H	1.00	-0.03	1.00	9.66	14.27	3092	0.999	-0.00	0.03	0.03	11.820	1.00	0.6	-0.0	WCA 2A	WCA 2A
S11C_H	P2	S11A_H	1.00	-0.02	1.00	—	—	3038	0.999	0.00	0.04	0.04	—	1.00	0.8	0.0	WCA 2A	WCA 2A
S11C_H	P3	S144_H	0.96	2.11	0.99	—	—	2848	0.973	-0.00	0.16	0.16	—	0.97	3.4	-0.0	WCA 2A	WCA 2A
S11C_H	P4	—	—	—	—	—	—	—	—	—	—	—	—	—	—	—	WCA 2A	—

Appendix 3. EDEN water-level estimation equations and performance statistics sorted by station name.—Continued

[n, number of data points; R², coefficient of determination; RMSE, root mean square error; WCA, Water Conservation Area; ENP, Everglades National Park; BCNP, Big Cypress National Preserve; FB, Florida Bay]

[a]Station name	[a]Predictor number	Predictor station name	Slope, m	y-intercept, b	Pearson correlation coefficient	[a]Minimum observed	[a]Maximum observed	n	R²	Mean error	RMSE	Standard error	[a]Average measured, in feet	Nash-Sutcliffe	Percent model error	Percent model bias	Area of site	Area of predictor
S11C_T	P1	S11B_T	1.01	-0.10	1.00	7.85	13.07	2941	0.999	0.00	0.04	0.04	10.094	1.00	0.8	0.0	WCA 3A	WCA 3A
S11C_T	P2	S11A_T	1.02	-0.16	1.00	—	—	2980	0.996	0.00	0.07	0.07	—	1.00	1.4	0.0	WCA 3A	WCA 3A
S11C_T	P3	S142_H	1.03	1.37	1.00	—	—	2786	0.992	0.00	0.10	0.10	—	0.99	1.9	0.0	WCA 3A	L38E Canal
S11C_T	P4	—	—	—	—	—	—	—	—	—	—	—	—	—	—	—	WCA 3A	—
S12A_H	P1	S12B_H	0.99	0.10	1.00	7.42	10.78	3110	0.997	-0.00	0.04	0.04	9.404	1.00	1.1	-0.0	Tamiami Canal	Tamiami Canal
S12A_H	P2	S12C_H	0.98	0.17	1.00	—	—	3077	0.996	-0.00	0.05	0.05	—	1.00	1.4	-0.1	Tamiami Canal	Tamiami Canal
S12A_H	P3	S343B_H	0.97	1.67	1.00	—	—	3005	0.995	-0.00	0.05	0.05	—	0.99	1.6	-0.0	Tamiami Canal	WCA 3A
S12A_H	P4	—	—	—	—	—	—	—	—	—	—	—	—	—	—	—	Tamiami Canal	—
S12A_T	P1	3A-5	1.28	-2.89	0.91	6.73	10.79	727	0.833	-0.01	0.27	0.24	8.397	0.84	6.5	-0.1	ENP	WCA 3A
S12A_T	P2	W18	1.10	-1.05	0.89	—	—	1573	0.795	-0.01	0.38	0.34	—	0.79	9.5	-0.1	ENP	WCA 3A
S12A_T	P3	EDEN_14	1.17	-1.89	0.88	—	—	677	0.781	-0.01	0.28	0.24	—	0.79	6.9	-0.1	ENP	WCA 3A
S12A_T	P4	—	—	—	—	—	—	—	—	—	—	—	—	—	—	—	ENP	—
S12B_H	P1	S12C_H	0.99	0.06	1.00	7.42	10.86	3086	0.997	-0.00	0.04	0.04	9.402	1.00	1.1	-0.0	Tamiami Canal	Tamiami Canal
S12B_H	P2	S12A_H	1.01	-0.07	1.00	—	—	3110	0.997	0.00	0.04	0.04	—	1.00	1.1	0.0	Tamiami Canal	Tamiami Canal
S12B_H	P3	S343B_H	0.98	1.61	1.00	—	—	3014	0.991	0.00	0.07	0.07	—	0.99	2.0	0.0	Tamiami Canal	WCA 3A
S12B_H	P4	—	—	—	—	—	—	—	—	—	—	—	—	—	—	—	Tamiami Canal	—
S12B_T	P1	S12C_T	0.94	0.41	0.97	6.69	10.85	3126	0.949	-0.00	0.23	0.23	8.471	0.95	5.6	-0.0	ENP	ENP
S12B_T	P2	W11	1.24	-1.86	0.91	—	—	1859	0.827	-0.00	0.42	0.38	—	0.83	10.1	-0.0	ENP	WCA 3A
S12B_T	P3	SITE_64	1.16	-3.22	0.90	—	—	3117	0.805	-0.00	0.46	0.41	—	0.80	11.0	-0.0	ENP	WCA 3A
S12B_T	P4	—	—	—	—	—	—	—	—	—	—	—	—	—	—	—	ENP	—
S12C_H	P1	S12B_H	1.00	-0.04	1.00	7.44	10.90	3086	0.997	0.00	0.04	0.04	9.402	1.00	1.1	0.0	Tamiami Canal	Tamiami Canal
S12C_H	P2	S12A_H	1.01	-0.11	1.00	—	—	3077	0.996	0.00	0.05	0.05	—	1.00	1.4	0.1	Tamiami Canal	Tamiami Canal
S12C_H	P3	S12D_H	0.95	0.42	1.00	—	—	3086	0.993	0.00	0.06	0.06	—	0.99	1.9	0.0	Tamiami Canal	Tamiami Canal
S12C_H	P4	—	—	—	—	—	—	—	—	—	—	—	—	—	—	—	Tamiami Canal	—

Appendix 3. EDEN water-level estimation equations and performance statistics sorted by station name.—Continued

[n, number of data points; R^2, coefficient of determination; RMSE, root mean square error; WCA, Water Conservation Area; ENP, Everglades National Park; BCNP, Big Cypress National Preserve; FB, Florida Bay]

Station name	Predictor number	Predictor station name	Slope, m	y-intercept, b	Pearson correlation coefficient	Minimum observed[a]	Maximum observed[a]	n	R^2	Mean error	RMSE	Standard error	Average measured, in feet[a]	Nash-Sutcliffe	Percent model error	Percent model bias	Area of site	Area of predictor
S12C_T	P1	S12B_T	1.00	0.03	0.97	6.70	10.90	3126	0.949	0.00	0.24	0.23	8.532	0.95	5.7	0.0	ENP	ENP
S12C_T	P2	W11	1.27	-2.09	0.92	—	—	1855	0.840	-0.00	0.41	0.38	—	0.84	9.7	-0.0	ENP	WCA 3A
S12C_T	P3	NP202	1.56	0.09	0.91	—	—	3130	0.829	-0.00	0.44	0.40	—	0.83	10.4	-0.0	ENP	ENP
S12C_T	P4	—	—	—	—	—	—		—	—	—	—	—	—	—	—	ENP	—
S12D_H	P1	S333_H	0.97	1.77	1.00	7.43	11.06	2918	0.998	0.00	0.04	0.04	9.461	1.00	1.0	0.0	Tamiami Canal	Tamiami Canal
S12D_H	P2	S12C_H	1.04	-0.37	1.00	—	—	3086	0.993	-0.00	0.07	0.07	—	0.99	1.8	-0.0	Tamiami Canal	Tamiami Canal
S12D_H	P3	S12B_H	1.05	-0.39	0.99	—	—	3118	0.987	-0.00	0.09	0.09	—	0.99	2.4	-0.0	Tamiami Canal	Tamiami Canal
S12D_H	P4	—	—	—	—	—	—		—	—	—	—	—	—	—	—	Tamiami Canal	—
S12D_T	P1	SITE_64	1.52	-6.66	0.90	5.49	11.02	3106	0.814	-0.00	0.58	0.52	8.619	0.81	10.5	-0.0	ENP	WCA 3A
S12D_T	P2	S9A_T	1.09	-0.42	0.90	—	—	2618	0.813	-0.00	0.58	0.52	—	0.81	10.4	-0.0	ENP	WCA 3B
S12D_T	P3	3A9	1.66	-6.70	0.90	—	—	3022	0.812	-0.00	0.59	0.53	—	0.81	10.6	-0.0	ENP	WCA 3A
S12D_T	P4	—	—	—	—	—	—		—	—	—	—	—	—	—	—	ENP	—
S140_H	P1	L28S1	1.03	-0.67	0.93	7.11	9.41	1991	0.857	-0.01	0.19	0.18	8.411	0.86	8.1	-0.1	L28 Canal	L28 Canal
S140_H	P2	G211_T	0.27	7.60	0.22	—	—	2014	0.048	0.00	0.48	0.10	—	0.05	20.7	0.0	L28 Canal	L31N Canal
S140_H	P3	S190_H	0.07	7.55	0.10	—	—	2012	0.009	0.00	0.49	0.05	—	0.01	21.1	0.0	L28 Canal North	L28 Canal North Feeder Canal
S140_H	P4	—	—	—	—	—	—		—	—	—	—	—	—	—	—	L28 Canal	—
S140_T	P1	SITE_62	1.31	-5.04	0.97	6.48	11.70	1966	0.936	0.00	0.26	0.25	9.450	0.94	5.0	0.0	WCA 3A	WCA 3A
S140_T	P2	S339_T	1.13	-1.01	0.96	—	—	1846	0.924	0.00	0.28	0.27	—	0.92	5.3	0.0	WCA 3A	Miami Canal
S140_T	P3	3AN1W1	1.43	-4.29	0.96	—	—	1845	0.918	0.00	0.30	0.29	—	0.92	5.7	0.0	WCA 3A	WCA 3A
S140_T	P4	—	—	—	—	—	—		—	—	—	—	—	—	—	—	WCA 3A	—
S141_H	P1	SITE_99	0.76	0.86	0.96	5.68	9.95	2643	0.921	-0.01	0.26	0.25	8.316	0.92	6.2	-0.1	WCA 2B	WCA 2B
S141_H	P2	EDEN_12	0.87	0.65	0.95	—	—	314	0.902	0.02	0.23	0.23	—	0.95	5.5	0.2	WCA 2B	WCA 3A
S141_H	P3	EDEN_13	1.32	-2.68	0.93	—	—	332	0.850	0.04	0.29	0.28	—	0.92	6.8	0.5	WCA 2B	WCA 2B
S141_H	P4	—	—	—	—	—	—		—	—	—	—	—	—	—	—	WCA 2B	—
S141_T	P1	S34_H	0.97	0.20	0.97	6.08	10.48	2640	0.949	0.00	0.20	0.19	8.247	0.95	4.5	0.0	L38E	L38E Canal
S141_T	P2	S143_T	0.97	0.39	0.97	—	—	2475	0.944	0.00	0.20	0.19	—	0.94	4.5	0.0	L38E	L38E Canal
S141_T	P3	S142_T	0.96	0.21	0.97	—	—	2377	0.940	0.00	0.21	0.21	—	0.94	4.8	0.0	L38E	WCA 3A
S141_T	P4	—	—	—	—	—	—		—	—	—	—	—	—	—	—	L38E Canal	—

[a] = superscript notation on Minimum observed, Maximum observed, and Average measured columns.

Appendix 3.   EDEN water-level estimation equations and performance statistics sorted by station name.—Continued

[n, number of data points; R², coefficient of determination; RMSE, root mean square error; WCA, Water Conservation Area; ENP, Everglades National Park; BCNP, Big Cypress National Preserve; FB, Florida Bay]

[a]Station name	[a]Predictor number	Predictor station name	Slope m	y-intercept, b	Pearson correlation coefficient	[a]Minimum observed	[a]Maximum observed	n	R²	Mean error	RMSE	Standard error	[a]Average measured, in feet	Nash-Sutcliffe	Percent model error	Percent model bias	Area of site	Area of predictor
S142_H	P1	S11A_T	0.99	-1.47	1.00	6.03	11.22	2881	0.997	-0.00	0.06	0.06	8.468	1.00	1.2	-0.0	L38E Canal	WCA 3A
S142_H	P2	S11B_T	0.98	-1.34	1.00	—	—	2749	0.995	-0.00	0.07	0.07	—	1.00	1.4	-0.0	L38E Canal	WCA 3A
S142_H	P3	S11C_T	0.97	-1.26	1.00	—	—	2786	0.992	-0.00	0.09	0.09	—	0.99	1.8	-0.0	L38E Canal	WCA 3A
S142_H	P4	—	—	—	—	—	—	—	—	—	—	—	—	—	—	—	L38E Canal	—
S142_T	P1	S34_H	1.00	0.11	0.99	5.90	10.68	2807	0.980	-0.00	0.13	0.13	8.259	0.98	2.7	-0.0	WCA 3A	L38E Canal
S142_T	P2	S143_T	0.99	0.33	0.98	—	—	2583	0.966	-0.00	0.16	0.15	—	0.97	3.3	-0.0	WCA 3A	L38E Canal
S142_T	P3	S141_T	0.98	0.29	0.97	—	—	2377	0.940	-0.01	0.22	0.21	—	0.94	4.5	-0.1	WCA 3A	L38E Canal
S142_T	P4	—	—	—	—	—	—	—	—	—	—	—	—	—	—	—	WCA 3A	—
S143_T	P1	S34_H	1.00	-0.08	0.99	5.93	10.42	2879	0.989	0.00	0.09	0.09	8.140	0.99	2.0	0.0	L38E Canal	L38E Canal
S143_T	P2	S142_T	0.98	-0.04	0.98	—	—	2583	0.966	-0.00	0.16	0.15	—	0.97	3.5	0.0	L38E Canal	WCA 3A
S143_T	P3	S141_T	0.98	0.08	0.97	—	—	2475	0.944	-0.00	0.20	0.19	—	0.94	4.5	-0.0	L38E Canal	L38E Canal
S143_T	P4	—	—	—	—	—	—	—	—	—	—	—	—	—	—	—	L38E Canal	—
S144_H	P1	S146_H	0.98	0.65	1.00	7.95	12.45	2229	0.992	-0.00	0.08	0.08	10.096	0.99	1.8	-0.0	WCA 2A	WCA 2A
S144_H	P2	S145_H	0.96	0.41	0.99	—	—	2610	0.975	0.00	0.15	0.15	—	0.97	3.4	0.0	WCA 2A	WCA 2A
S144_H	P3	S11A_H	1.02	-1.89	0.99	—	—	2834	0.974	0.00	0.16	0.16	—	0.97	3.6	0.0	WCA 2A	WCA 2A
S144_H	P4	—	—	—	—	—	—	—	—	—	—	—	—	—	—	—	WCA 2A	—
S144_T	P1	S145_T	1.00	0.09	0.93	3.37	10.35	2457	0.859	0.00	0.23	0.22	9.098	0.86	3.3	0.0	WCA 2B	WCA 2B
S144_T	P2	S146_T	0.95	0.71	0.87	—	—	2341	0.779	0.00	0.29	0.25	—	0.78	4.2	0.1	WCA 2B	WCA 2B
S144_T	P3	EDEN_11	0.78	0.15	0.63	—	—	758	0.403	0.01	0.50	0.32	—	0.43	7.2	0.1	WCA 2B	WCA 2A
S144_T	P4	—	—	—	—	—	—	—	—	—	—	—	—	—	—	—	WCA 2B	—
S145_H	P1	S146_H	0.99	0.53	0.99	7.88	12.71	2223	0.984	0.00	0.12	0.12	10.128	0.98	2.5	0.0	WCA 2A	WCA 2A
S145_H	P2	S144_H	1.02	-0.17	0.99	—	—	2610	0.975	0.00	0.16	0.16	—	0.97	3.3	0.0	WCA 2A	WCA 2A
S145_H	P3	SITE_17	1.20	-4.53	0.96	—	—	2711	0.925	0.00	0.28	0.27	—	0.92	5.7	0.0	WCA 2A	WCA 2A
S145_H	P4	—	—	—	—	—	—	—	—	—	—	—	—	—	—	—	WCA 2A	—
S145_T	P1	S146_T	0.95	0.67	0.94	7.82	10.08	2308	0.892	0.00	0.19	0.18	9.017	0.89	8.3	0.0	WCA 2B	WCA 2B
S145_T	P2	S144_T	0.86	1.16	0.93	—	—	2457	0.859	-0.00	0.22	0.20	—	0.86	9.6	-0.0	WCA 2B	WCA 2B
S145_T	P3	S9A_T	0.36	6.00	0.71	—	—	2126	0.509	0.00	0.41	0.29	—	0.51	18.0	0.0	WCA 2B	WCA 3B
S145_T	P4	—	—	—	—	—	—	—	—	—	—	—	—	—	—	—	WCA 2B	—

Appendix 3. EDEN water-level estimation equations and performance statistics sorted by station name.—Continued

[n, number of data points; R², coefficient of determination; RMSE, root mean square error; WCA, Water Conservation Area; ENP, Everglades National Park; BCNP, Big Cypress National Preserve; FB, Florida Bay]

[a]Station name	[a]Predictor number	Predictor station name	Slope, m	y-intercept, b	Pearson correlation coefficient	[a]Minimum observed	[a]Maximum observed	n	R²	Mean error	RMSE	Standard error	[a]Average measured, in feet	Nash-Sutcliffe	Percent model error	Percent model bias	Area of site	Area of predictor
S146_H	P1	S144_H	1.02	−0.58	1.00	7.49	11.81	2229	0.992	0.00	0.08	0.08	9.680	0.99	1.9	0.0	WCA 2A	WCA 2A
S146_H	P2	S145_H	0.99	−0.37	0.99	—	—	2223	0.984	−0.00	0.12	0.12	—	0.98	2.9	−0.0	WCA 2A	WCA 2A
S146_H	P3	S11A_H	1.02	−2.34	0.98	—	—	2338	0.952	0.00	0.21	0.21	—	0.95	4.9	0.0	WCA 2A	WCA 2A
S146_H	P4	—	—	—	—	—	—	—	—	—	—	—	—	—	—	—	WCA 2A	—
S146_T	P1	S145_T	0.94	0.32	0.94	7.53	10.21	2308	0.892	−0.00	0.19	0.18	8.823	0.89	7.0	−0.0	WCA 2B	WCA 2B
S146_T	P2	S144_T	0.79	1.59	0.87	—	—	2341	0.779	−0.00	0.26	0.23	—	0.78	9.8	−0.0	WCA 2B	WCA 2B
S146_T	P3	EDEN_11	0.87	−1.08	0.77	—	—	560	0.672	−0.01	0.29	0.24	—	0.67	11.0	−0.1	WCA 2B	WCA 2A
S146_T	P4	—	—	—	—	—	—	—	—	—	—	—	—	—	—	—	WCA 2B	—
S150_T	P1	EDEN_5	1.53	−5.12	0.98	6.16	11.13	538	0.726	0.14	0.54	0.39	8.846	0.70	10.8	1.6	WCA 3A	WCA 3A
S150_T	P2	EDEN_9	1.28	−2.65	0.98	—	—	528	0.565	0.25	0.71	0.53	—	0.52	14.3	2.8	WCA 3A	WCA 3A
S150_T	P3	S11C_T	0.95	−0.96	0.98	—	—	1198	0.879	0.04	0.40	0.38	—	0.88	8.1	0.5	WCA 3A	WCA 3A
S150_T	P4	—	—	—	—	—	—	—	—	—	—	—	—	—	—	—	WCA 3A	—
S151_H	P1	S9A_T	0.95	0.23	0.99	5.91	10.49	2357	0.987	−0.00	0.12	0.12	8.105	0.99	2.7	−0.0	Miami Canal	WCA 3B
S151_H	P2	S340_T	0.93	0.35	0.99	—	—	2750	0.978	0.00	0.16	0.16	—	0.98	3.4	0.0	Miami Canal	Miami Canal
S151_H	P3	S11A_T	0.89	−0.69	0.99	—	—	2848	0.975	−0.00	0.17	0.16	—	0.97	3.6	−0.0	Miami Canal	WCA 3A
S151_H	P4	—	—	—	—	—	—	—	—	—	—	—	—	—	—	—	Miami Canal	—
S151_T	P1	EDEN_7	1.13	−0.61	0.96	3.33	7.62	794	0.911	−0.01	0.14	0.13	6.171	0.93	3.2	−0.2	Miami Canal	WCA 3B
S151_T	P2	S31_H	1.01	0.14	0.99	—	—	2655	0.985	0.00	0.08	0.08	—	0.98	1.9	0.0	Miami Canal	Miami Canal
S151_T	P3	SITE_76	1.28	−3.56	0.91	—	—	2949	0.821	−0.00	0.29	0.26	—	0.82	6.8	−0.0	Miami Canal	WCA 3B
S151_T	P4	—	—	—	—	—	—	—	—	—	—	—	—	—	—	—	Miami Canal	—
S175_H	P1	L31W	1.00	−0.03	1.00	0.21	4.95	3021	0.998	−0.00	0.05	0.05	2.731	1.00	1.0	−0.0	L31W Canal	ENP
S175_H	P2	NTS1	0.98	0.06	0.99	—	—	3113	0.970	0.00	0.19	0.19	—	0.97	4.0	0.0	L31W Canal	ENP
S175_H	P3	NTS18	1.05	−0.22	0.99	—	—	3065	0.981	−0.00	0.15	0.15	—	0.98	3.1	−0.0	L31W Canal	ENP
S175_H	P4	—	—	—	—	—	—	—	—	—	—	—	—	—	—	—	L31W Canal	—

Appendix 3. EDEN water-level estimation equations and performance statistics sorted by station name.—Continued

[n, number of data points; R², coefficient of determination; RMSE, root mean square error; WCA, Water Conservation Area; ENP, Everglades National Park; BCNP, Big Cypress National Preserve; FB, Florida Bay]

[a]Station name	[a]Predictor number	Predictor station name	Slope, m	y-intercept, b	Pearson correlation coefficient	[a]Minimum observed	[a]Maximum observed	n	R²	Mean error	RMSE	Standard error	[a]Average measured, in feet	Nash-Sutcliffe	Percent model error	Percent model bias	Area of site	Area of predictor
S175_T	P1	TSB	0.50	0.02	0.97	-0.93	3.26	1787	0.934	-0.00	0.15	0.15	0.933	0.93	3.6	-0.0	L31W Canal	ENP
S175_T	P2	R127	0.80	0.42	0.97	—	—	3108	0.950	0.00	0.13	0.12	—	0.95	3.0	0.2	L31W Canal	ENP
S175_T	P3	EVER4	1.10	-1.23	0.97	—	—	3039	0.939	0.00	0.13	0.13	—	0.94	3.1	0.0	L31W Canal	ENP
S175_T	P4	—	—	—	—	—	—	—	—	—	—	—	—	—	—	—	L31W Canal	—
S18C_T	P1	CT50R	1.03	1.60	1.00	0.18	3.32	2991	0.993	0.00	0.04	0.04	1.902	0.99	1.3	0.0	C111 Canal	ENP
S18C_T	P2	CT27R	1.03	1.40	0.99	—	—	3002	0.987	0.00	0.06	0.06	—	0.99	1.8	0.0	C111 Canal	ENP
S18C_T	P3	EVER6	1.14	1.37	0.98	—	—	3021	0.970	-0.00	0.09	0.09	—	0.97	2.9	-0.1	C111 Canal	ENP
S18C_T	P4	—	—	—	—	—	—	—	—	—	—	—	—	—	—	—	C111 Canal	—
S190_H	P1	BCA13	0.74	5.08	0.72	9.16	14.71	3056	0.506	-0.02	0.72	0.52	13.066	0.51	12.9	-0.1	North Feeder Canal	BCNP
S190_H	P2	BCA11	0.69	10.90	0.75	—	—	2837	0.560	-0.02	0.69	0.52	—	0.56	12.4	-0.1	North Feeder Canal	BCNP
S190_H	P3	S10A_H	0.83	-0.15	0.73	—	—	3091	0.527	0.00	0.69	0.50	—	0.53	12.5	0.0	North Feeder Canal	L39 Canal
S190_H	P4	—	—	—	—	—	—	—	—	—	—	—	—	—	—	—	North Feeder Canal	—
S190_T	P1	L28S2	1.08	-0.84	0.92	7.17	12.91	3124	0.747	0.03	0.40	0.36	9.622	0.75	7.0	0.3	L28 Interceptor Canal	L28 Canal
S190_T	P2	S140_T	0.76	2.49	0.91	—	—	1980	0.825	0.00	0.36	0.32	—	0.83	6.2	0.0	L28 Interceptor Canal	WCA 3A
S190_T	P3	3AN1W1	1.12	-1.04	0.89	—	—	1896	0.793	0.00	0.40	0.35	—	0.79	6.9	0.0	L28 Interceptor Canal	WCA 3A
S190_T	P4	—	—	—	—	—	—	—	—	—	—	—	—	—	—	—	L28 Interceptor Canal	—

Appendix 3. EDEN water-level estimation equations and performance statistics sorted by station name.—Continued

[n, number of data points; R^2, coefficient of determination; RMSE, root mean square error; WCA, Water Conservation Area; ENP, Everglades National Park; BCNP, Big Cypress National Preserve; FB, Florida Bay]

[a]Station name	[a]Predictor number	Predictor station name	Slope, m	y-intercept, b	Pearson correlation coefficient	[a]Minimum observed	[a]Maximum observed	n	R^2	Mean error	RMSE	Standard error	[a]Average measured, in feet	Nash-Sutcliffe	Percent model error	Percent model bias	Area of site	Area of predictor
S31_H	P1	S151_T	0.97	−0.05	0.99	3.22	7.38	2655	0.985	−0.00	0.08	0.08	5.919	0.98	1.9	−0.0	Miami Canal	Miami Canal
S31_H	P2	EDEN_7	1.13	−0.84	0.95	—	—	803	0.898	−0.00	0.15	0.14	—	0.91	3.6	−0.0	Miami Canal	WCA 3B
S31_H	P3	SITE_76	1.31	−3.91	0.90	—	—	2716	0.805	−0.00	0.29	0.26	—	0.80	7.0	−0.0	Miami Canal	WCA 3B
S31_H	P4	—	—	—	—	—	—	—	—	—	—	—	—	—	—	—	Miami Canal	—
S332_T	P1	TSB	0.74	1.64	0.94	2.06	4.91	1335	0.876	0.00	0.28	0.26	3.053	0.88	9.7	0.0	ENP	ENP
S332_T	P2	E112	0.71	1.16	0.92	—	—	2466	0.836	0.00	0.32	0.29	—	0.84	11.2	0.1	ENP	ENP
S332_T	P3	NTS1	0.69	1.04	0.91	—	—	2440	0.834	0.00	0.32	0.29	—	0.83	11.3	0.0	ENP	ENP
S332_T	P4	—	—	—	—	—	—	—	—	—	—	—	—	—	—	—	ENP	—
S332B_T	P1	NTS18	1.17	1.09	0.84	2.61	6.95	1707	0.705	−0.01	0.70	0.57	4.826	0.71	16.1	−0.2	ENP	ENP
S332B_T	P2	S175_H	1.12	1.36	0.84	—	—	1772	0.703	−0.01	0.70	0.57	—	0.70	16.2	−0.3	ENP	L31W Canal
S332B_T	P3	RG2	1.16	0.17	0.83	—	—	1758	0.689	−0.00	0.72	0.59	—	0.69	16.7	−0.1	ENP	ENP
S332B_T	P4	—	—	—	—	—	—	—	—	—	—	—	—	—	—	—	ENP	—
S332D_T	P1	NTS18	1.96	−1.52	0.88	0.34	7.57	3067	0.774	0.00	1.09	0.96	3.951	0.77	15.0	0.0	L31W Canal	ENP
S332D_T	P2	L31W	1.73	−0.83	0.84	—	—	3019	0.710	0.00	1.22	1.03	—	0.71	16.9	0.0	L31W Canal	ENP
S332D_T	P3	S175_H	1.73	−0.78	0.84	—	—	3121	0.700	0.00	1.24	1.04	—	0.70	17.1	0.0	L31W Canal	L31W Canal
S332D_T	P4	—	—	—	—	—	—	—	—	—	—	—	—	—	—	—	L31W Canal	—
S333_H	P1	S12D_H	1.03	−1.80	1.00	5.88	9.54	2918	0.998	−0.00	0.04	0.04	7.907	1.00	1.1	−0.0	Tamiami Canal	Tamiami Canal
S333_H	P2	S12C_H	1.07	−2.15	1.00	—	—	2886	0.992	−0.00	0.07	0.07	—	0.99	1.9	−0.0	Tamiami Canal	Tamiami Canal
S333_H	P3	S12B_H	1.07	−2.17	0.99	—	—	2929	0.986	0.00	0.09	0.09	—	0.99	2.6	0.0	Tamiami Canal	Tamiami Canal
S333_H	P4	—	—	—	—	—	—	—	—	—	—	—	—	—	—	—	Tamiami Canal	—
S333_T	P1	S334_H	1.05	−0.13	0.99	3.16	6.99	3036	0.984	−0.00	0.06	0.06	5.539	0.98	1.6	−0.0	Tamiami Canal	Tamiami Canal
S333_T	P2	L31NN	0.40	3.61	0.90	—	—	1287	0.819	0.00	0.19	0.17	—	0.84	4.9	0.0	Tamiami Canal	L31N Canal
S333_T	P3	NESRS3	0.46	3.20	0.90	—	—	2819	0.803	0.00	0.21	0.18	—	0.80	5.4	0.0	Tamiami Canal	ENP
S333_T	P4	—	—	—	—	—	—	—	—	—	—	—	—	—	—	—	Tamiami Canal	—

Appendix 3. EDEN water-level estimation equations and performance statistics sorted by station name.—Continued

[n, number of data points; R², coefficient of determination; RMSE, root mean square error; WCA, Water Conservation Area; ENP, Everglades National Park; BCNP, Big Cypress National Preserve; FB, Florida Bay]

[a]Station name	[a]Predictor number	Predictor station name	Slope, m	y-intercept, b	Pearson correlation coefficient	[a]Minimum observed	[a]Maximum observed	n	R²	Mean error	RMSE	Standard error	[a]Average measured, in feet	Nash-Sutcliffe	Percent model error	Percent model bias	Area of site	Area of predictor
S334_H	P1	S333_T	0.94	0.20	0.99	3.13	7.22	3036	0.984	0.00	0.06	0.06	5.412	0.98	1.4	0.0	Tamiami Canal	Tamiami Canal
S334_H	P2	L31NN	0.38	3.59	0.90	—	—	1337	0.804	0.00	0.19	0.17	—	0.82	4.6	0.0	Tamiami Canal	L31N Canal
S334_H	P3	NESRS3	0.44	3.19	0.90	—	—	2853	0.803	0.00	0.19	0.17	—	0.80	4.7	0.0	Tamiami Canal	ENP
S334_H	P4	—	—	—	—	—	—	—	—	—	—	—	—	—	—	—	Tamiami Canal	—
S334_T	P1	L31N_1	1.00	-1.74	1.00	1.91	5.97	3040	0.995	0.00	0.04	0.04	3.882	1.00	1.0	0.0	Tamiami Canal	L31N Canal
S334_T	P2	L31N_3	1.01	-1.80	1.00	—	—	3031	0.994	0.00	0.04	0.04	—	0.99	1.1	0.0	Tamiami Canal	L31N Canal
S334_T	P3	S335_T	1.01	0.12	1.00	—	—	3032	0.993	-0.00	0.05	0.05	—	0.99	1.2	-0.0	Tamiami Canal	L30 Canal
S334_T	P4	—	—	—	—	—	—	—	—	—	—	—	—	—	—	—	Tamiami Canal	—
S335_H	P1	S337_T	1.02	-0.22	1.00	1.88	6.19	2864	0.991	-0.00	0.07	0.07	4.303	0.99	1.6	-0.0	L30 Canal	L30 Canal
S335_H	P2	3BS1W1	0.79	0.31	0.91	—	—	2667	0.822	0.00	0.31	0.28	—	0.82	7.3	0.0	L30 Canal	WCA 3B
S335_H	P3	S336_T	1.02	0.29	0.89	—	—	2939	0.791	0.00	0.36	0.32	—	0.79	8.3	0.0	L30 Canal	Tamiami Canal
S335_H	P4	—	—	—	—	—	—	—	—	—	—	—	—	—	—	—	L30 Canal	—
S335_T	P1	S336_H	0.98	0.08	1.00	1.81	5.85	3040	0.993	0.00	0.05	0.05	3.707	0.99	1.2	0.0	L30 Canal	Tamiami Canal
S335_T	P2	S334_T	0.98	-0.09	1.00	—	—	3032	0.993	0.00	0.05	0.05	—	0.99	1.2	0.0	L30 Canal	Tamiami Canal
S335_T	P3	L31N_1	0.99	-1.83	1.00	—	—	3103	0.997	0.00	0.03	0.03	—	1.00	0.8	0.0	L30 Canal	L31N Canal
S335_T	P4	—	—	—	—	—	—	—	—	—	—	—	—	—	—	—	L30 Canal	—
S336_H	P1	L31N_1	1.01	-1.93	1.00	1.83	5.89	3050	0.995	0.00	0.04	0.04	3.705	0.99	1.0	0.0	Tamiami Canal	L31N Canal
S336_H	P2	S335_T	1.02	-0.06	1.00	—	—	3040	0.993	-0.00	0.05	0.05	—	0.99	1.2	-0.0	Tamiami Canal	L30 Canal
S336_H	P3	L31N_4	1.01	-1.98	1.00	—	—	3053	0.993	0.00	0.05	0.05	—	0.99	1.2	0.0	Tamiami Canal	L31N Canal
S336_H	P4	—	—	—	—	—	—	—	—	—	—	—	—	—	—	—	Tamiami Canal	—

Appendix 3. EDEN water-level estimation equations and performance statistics sorted by station name.—Continued

[n, number of data points; R², coefficient of determination; RMSE, root mean square error; WCA, Water Conservation Area; ENP, Everglades National Park; BCNP, Big Cypress National Preserve; FB, Florida Bay]

[a]Station name	[a]Predictor number	Predictor station name	Slope, m	y-intercept, b	Pearson correlation coefficient	[a]Minimum observed	[a]Maximum observed	n	R²	Mean error	RMSE	Standard error	[a]Average measured, in feet	Nash-Sutcliffe	Percent model error	Percent model bias	Area of site	Area of predictor
S336_T	P1	L31NN	0.64	0.87	0.96	1.84	5.29	1326	0.922	−0.00	0.19	0.18	3.902	0.93	5.5	−0.0	Tamiami Canal	L31N Canal
S336_T	P2	S336_H	1.09	−0.14	0.95	—	—	3011	0.895	−0.00	0.22	0.21	—	0.89	6.5	−0.0	Tamiami Canal	Tamiami Canal
S336_T	P3	3BS1W1	0.72	0.26	0.95	—	—	2740	0.903	−0.00	0.21	0.20	—	0.90	6.0	−0.0	Tamiami Canal	WCA 3B
S336_T	P4	—	—	—	—	—	—	—	—	—	—	—	—	—	—	—	Tamiami Canal	—
S337_T	P1	S335_H	0.97	0.25	1.00	2.04	6.32	2864	0.991	0.00	0.07	0.07	4.412	0.99	1.6	0.0	L30 Canal	L30 Canal
S337_T	P2	3BS1W1	0.74	0.69	0.90	—	—	2676	0.815	0.00	0.30	0.28	—	0.82	7.1	0.0	L30 Canal	WCA 3B
S337_T	P3	3BS1W1	0.74	0.69	0.90	—	—	2676	0.815	0.00	0.30	0.28	—	0.82	7.1	0.0	L30 Canal	WCA 3B
S337_T	P4	—	—	—	—	—	—	—	—	—	—	—	—	—	—	—	L30 Canal	—
S339_H	P1	S8_T	0.66	2.13	0.93	6.24	11.27	2922	0.866	−0.00	0.34	0.31	9.739	0.87	6.7	−0.0	Miami Canal	Miami Canal
S339_H	P2	S140_T	0.69	3.35	0.86	—	—	1934	0.747	−0.00	0.42	0.36	—	0.75	8.3	−0.0	Miami Canal	WCA 3A
S339_H	P3	3ANW	0.96	0.22	0.86	—	—	2015	0.745	−0.01	0.39	0.33	—	0.75	7.7	−0.1	Miami Canal	WCA 3A
S339_H	P4	—	—	—	—	—	—	—	—	—	—	—	—	—	—	—	Miami Canal	—
S339_T	P1	3AN1W1	1.25	−2.67	0.96	6.19	11.06	1784	0.922	−0.00	0.24	0.23	9.148	0.92	5.0	−0.0	Miami Canal	WCA 3A
S339_T	P2	S340_H	1.01	−0.06	0.97	—	—	2835	0.939	0.00	0.21	0.21	—	0.94	4.4	0.0	Miami Canal	Miami Canal
S339_T	P3	S140_T	0.82	1.52	0.96	—	—	1846	0.924	−0.00	0.24	0.23	—	0.92	4.8	−0.0	Miami Canal	WCA 3A
S339_T	P4	—	—	—	—	—	—	—	—	—	—	—	—	—	—	—	Miami Canal	—
S34_H	P1	S143_T	0.99	0.17	0.99	5.79	10.51	2879	0.989	−0.00	0.09	0.09	8.177	0.99	1.9	−0.0	L38E Canal	L38E Canal
S34_H	P2	S142_T	0.98	0.06	0.99	—	—	2807	0.980	0.00	0.13	0.12	—	0.98	2.7	0.0	L38E Canal	WCA 3A
S34_H	P3	S141_T	0.97	0.23	0.97	—	—	2640	0.949	−0.00	0.20	0.19	—	0.95	4.2	−0.0	L38E Canal	L38E Canal
S34_H	P4	—	—	—	—	—	—	—	—	—	—	—	—	—	—	—	L38E Canal	—

Appendix 3. EDEN water-level estimation equations and performance statistics sorted by station name.—Continued

[n, number of data points; R², coefficient of determination; RMSE, root mean square error; WCA, Water Conservation Area; ENP, Everglades National Park; BCNP, Big Cypress National Preserve; FB, Florida Bay]

[a]Station name	[a]Predictor number	Predictor station name	Slope, m	y-intercept, b	Pearson correlation coefficient	[a]Minimum observed	[a]Maximum observed	n	R²	Mean error	RMSE	Standard error	[a]Average measured, in feet	Nash-Sutcliffe	Percent model error	Percent model bias	Area of site	Area of predictor
S340_H	P1	3A9	1.03	-0.34	0.94	6.33	10.96	2930	0.876	-0.00	0.29	0.27	9.153	0.88	6.2	-0.0	Miami Canal	WCA 3A
S340_H	P2	S339_T	0.93	0.61	0.97	—	—	2835	0.939	-0.00	0.21	0.20	—	0.94	4.4	-0.0	Miami Canal	Miami Canal
S340_H	P3	S140_T	0.77	1.87	0.94	—	—	1953	0.887	-0.00	0.28	0.27	—	0.89	6.1	-0.0	Miami Canal	WCA 3A
S340_H	P4	—	—	—	—	—	—	—	—	—	—	—	—	—	—	—	Miami Canal	—
S340_T	P1	S151_H	1.06	-0.18	0.99	4.75	10.94	2750	0.978	-0.00	0.17	0.17	8.442	0.98	2.7	-0.0	Miami Canal	Miami Canal
S340_T	P2	S150_T	0.94	0.35	0.97	—	—	1190	0.758	-0.15	0.58	0.54	—	0.73	9.4	-1.7	Miami Canal	WCA 3A
S340_T	P3	S9A_T	1.02	-0.07	0.96	—	—	2490	0.951	0.01	0.26	0.25	—	0.95	4.2	0.1	Miami Canal	WCA 3B
S340_T	P4	—	—	—	—	—	—	—	—	—	—	—	—	—	—	—	Miami Canal	—
S343A_H	P1	S343B_H	1.00	0.03	1.00	5.99	9.35	2506	0.994	0.00	0.06	0.06	7.931	0.99	1.7	0.0	WCA 3A	WCA 3A
S343A_H	P2	S12B_H	1.01	-1.57	0.99	—	—	2542	0.990	0.00	0.08	0.08	—	0.99	2.3	0.0	WCA 3A	Tamiami Canal
S343A_H	P3	S12A_H	1.02	-1.64	0.99	—	—	2532	0.994	0.01	0.06	0.06	—	0.99	1.8	0.1	WCA 3A	Tamiami Canal
S343A_H	P4	—	—	—	—	—	—	—	—	—	—	—	—	—	—	—	WCA 3A	—
S343A_T	P1	S343B_T	1.10	-0.63	0.99	4.95	8.60	2661	0.977	0.00	0.08	0.08	7.064	0.98	2.2	0.0	L28 Canal	L28 Canal
S343A_T	P2	S344_T	0.72	1.43	0.96	—	—	2496	0.921	0.00	0.15	0.15	—	0.92	4.1	0.0	L28 Canal	BCNP
S343A_T	P3	LOOP1_H	0.93	1.37	0.93	—	—	2517	0.836	0.01	0.21	0.20	—	0.84	5.7	0.1	L28 Canal	BCNP
S343A_T	P4	—	—	—	—	—	—	—	—	—	—	—	—	—	—	—	L28 Canal	—
S343B_H	P1	S12A_H	1.02	-1.64	1.00	5.95	10.22	3005	0.995	0.00	0.06	0.06	7.938	0.99	1.3	0.1	WCA 3A	Tamiami Canal
S343B_H	P2	S343A_H	0.99	0.04	1.00	—	—	2506	0.994	-0.00	0.06	0.06	—	0.99	1.4	-0.0	WCA 3A	WCA 3A
S343B_H	P3	S12B_H	1.01	-1.56	1.00	—	—	3014	0.991	-0.00	0.07	0.07	—	0.99	1.7	-0.0	WCA 3A	Tamiami Canal
S343B_H	P4	—	—	—	—	—	—	—	—	—	—	—	—	—	—	—	WCA 3A	—
S343B_T	P1	S343A_T	0.89	0.74	0.99	4.96	8.42	2661	0.977	-0.00	0.07	0.07	7.013	0.98	2.1	-0.0	L28 Canal	L28 Canal
S343B_T	P2	LOOP1_H	0.84	1.83	0.92	—	—	2703	0.810	0.01	0.19	0.18	—	0.81	5.6	0.1	L28 Canal	BCNP
S343B_T	P3	S344_T	0.64	2.04	0.94	—	—	2516	0.888	0.00	0.16	0.15	—	0.89	4.6	0.0	L28 Canal	BCNP
S343B_T	P4	—	—	—	—	—	—	—	—	—	—	—	—	—	—	—	L28 Canal	—

Appendix 3. EDEN water-level estimation equations and performance statistics sorted by station name.—Continued

[n, number of data points; R², coefficient of determination; RMSE, root mean square error; WCA, Water Conservation Area; ENP, Everglades National Park; BCNP, Big Cypress National Preserve; FB, Florida Bay]

[a]Station name	[a]Predictor number	Predictor station name	Slope, m	y-intercept, b	Pearson correlation coefficient	[a]Minimum observed	[a]Maximum observed	n	R²	Mean error	RMSE	Standard error	[a]Average measured, in feet	Nash-Sutcliffe	Percent model error	Percent model bias	Area of site	Area of predictor
S344_H	P1	3ASW	1.02	-0.22	0.98	5.76	10.24	2677	0.964	-0.00	0.15	0.14	8.600	0.96	3.3	-0.0	WCA 3A	WCA 3A
S344_H	P2	S344_T	1.13	-0.26	0.96	—	—	2610	0.929	-0.00	0.22	0.21	—	0.93	4.9	-0.0	WCA 3A	BCNP
S344_H	P3	W11	1.07	-0.41	0.95	—	—	1475	0.910	-0.00	0.25	0.24	—	0.91	5.5	-0.0	WCA 3A	WCA 3A
S344_H	P4	—	—	—	—	—	—	—	—	—	—	—	—	—	—	—	WCA 3A	—
S344_T	P1	W11	0.88	0.40	0.97	5.11	9.43	1470	0.935	0.00	0.18	0.17	7.852	0.94	4.1	0.0	BCNP	WCA 3A
S344_T	P2	S344_H	0.82	0.77	0.96	—	—	2610	0.929	0.00	0.19	0.18	—	0.93	4.4	0.0	BCNP	WCA 3A
S344_T	P3	3ASW	0.85	0.51	0.96	—	—	2638	0.924	0.00	0.19	0.18	—	0.92	4.3	0.0	BCNP	WCA 3A
S344_T	P4	—	—	—	—	—	—	—	—	—	—	—	—	—	—	—	BCNP	—
S380_H	P1	S332B_T	0.48	0.53	0.83	1.23	4.90	1181	0.683	-0.00	0.40	0.33	2.551	0.68	10.9	-0.1	Pennsuco Wetlands	ENP
S380_H	P2	TSB	0.54	1.48	0.86	—	—	153	0.739	-0.00	0.29	0.25	—	0.77	8.0	-0.0	Pennsuco Wetlands	ENP
S380_H	P3	S150_T	0.52	-2.04	0.81	—	—	1212	0.584	-0.03	0.45	0.39	—	0.57	12.4	-1.2	Pennsuco Wetlands	WCA 3A
S380_H	P4	—	—	—	—	—	—	—	—	—	—	—	—	—	—	—	Pennsuco Wetlands	—
S39_H	P1	S10C_H	1.02	-2.06	0.99	10.00	15.97	2596	0.980	0.00	0.13	0.13	14.258	0.98	2.2	0.0	L39 Canal	L39 Canal
S39_H	P2	S10A_H	1.01	-1.94	0.99	—	—	2560	0.976	0.00	0.14	0.14	—	0.98	2.4	0.0	L39 Canal	L39 Canal
S39_H	P3	S10D_H	1.02	-2.05	0.99	—	—	2586	0.975	0.00	0.14	0.13	—	0.97	2.3	0.0	L39 Canal	L39 Canal
S39_H	P4	—	—	—	—	—	—	—	—	—	—	—	—	—	—	—	L39 Canal	—
S7_T	P1	SITE_17	1.39	-6.24	0.87	8.13	14.15	3072	0.753	0.00	0.65	0.57	10.693	0.75	10.9	0.0	L38E Canal	WCA 2A
S7_T	P2	S145_H	1.13	-0.75	0.88	—	—	2773	0.768	0.00	0.63	0.55	—	0.77	10.4	0.0	L38E Canal	WCA 2A
S7_T	P3	S144_H	1.15	-0.94	0.87	—	—	2877	0.761	0.00	0.64	0.56	—	0.76	10.6	0.0	L38E Canal	WCA 2A
S7_T	P4	—	—	—	—	—	—	—	—	—	—	—	—	—	—	—	L38E Canal	—
S8_T	P1	S339_H	1.30	-1.21	0.93	7.80	15.03	2922	0.866	0.00	0.47	0.44	11.478	0.87	6.5	0.0	Miami Canal	Miami Canal
S8_T	P2	3A10	1.77	-5.80	0.88	—	—	2073	0.786	0.02	0.56	0.50	—	0.79	7.8	0.2	Miami Canal	WCA 3A
S8_T	P3	S140_T	1.02	2.00	0.82	—	—	1984	0.681	0.00	0.71	0.58	—	0.68	9.8	0.0	Miami Canal	WCA 3A
S8_T	P4	—	—	—	—	—	—	—	—	—	—	—	—	—	—	—	Miami Canal	—

Appendix 3. EDEN water-level estimation equations and performance statistics sorted by station name.—Continued

[n, number of data points; R², coefficient of determination; RMSE, root mean square error; WCA, Water Conservation Area; ENP, Everglades National Park; BCNP, Big Cypress National Preserve; FB, Florida Bay]

[a]Station name	[a]Predictor number	Predictor station name	Slope, m	y-intercept, b	Pearson correlation coefficient	[a]Minimum observed	[a]Maximum observed	n	R²	Mean error	RMSE	Standard error	[a]Average measured, in feet	Nash-Sutcliffe	Percent model error	Percent model bias	Area of site	Area of predictor
S9A_T	P1	S151_H	1.04	-0.13	0.99	5.92	10.73	2357	0.987	-0.00	0.13	0.13	8.428	0.99	2.7	-0.0	WCA 3B	Miami Canal
S9A_T	P2	S142_H	0.94	0.34	0.99	—	—	2431	0.980	0.00	0.16	0.15	—	0.98	3.3	0.0	WCA 3B	L38E Canal
S9A_T	P3	S11A_T	0.93	-0.94	0.99	—	—	2586	0.979	0.00	0.16	0.16	—	0.98	3.4	0.0	WCA 3B	WCA 3A
S9A_T	P4	—	—	—	—	—	—	—	—	—	—	—	—	—	—	—	WCA 3B	—
SITE_17	P1	SITE_19	0.90	1.27	0.98	10.29	14.60	2965	0.954	-0.00	0.17	0.17	12.188	0.95	4.0	-0.0	WCA 2A	WCA 2A
SITE_17	P2	S146_H	0.78	4.63	0.97	—	—	2315	0.937	-0.00	0.20	0.19	—	0.94	4.5	-0.0	WCA 2A	WCA 2A
SITE_17	P3	S145_H	0.77	4.39	0.96	—	—	2711	0.925	-0.00	0.22	0.21	—	0.92	5.1	-0.0	WCA 2A	WCA 2A
SITE_17	P4	—	—	—	—	—	—	—	—	—	—	—	—	—	—	—	WCA 2A	—
SITE_19	P1	WCA2U1	0.95	2.17	0.98	10.83	14.62	2407	0.961	0.00	0.15	0.15	12.106	0.96	4.0	0.0	WCA 2A	WCA 2A
SITE_19	P2	WCA2U3	1.09	0.38	0.98	—	—	2645	0.959	0.01	0.18	0.17	—	0.96	4.7	0.1	WCA 2A	WCA 2A
SITE_19	P3	SITE_17	1.06	-0.78	0.98	—	—	2965	0.954	0.00	0.19	0.18	—	0.95	5.0	0.0	WCA 2A	WCA 2A
SITE_19	P4	—	—	—	—	—	—	—	—	—	—	—	—	—	—	—	WCA 2A	—
SITE_62	P1	3AN1W1	1.10	0.60	0.99	8.67	12.78	1882	0.971	-0.00	0.13	0.13	11.011	0.97	3.2	-0.0	WCA 3A	WCA 3A
SITE_62	P2	3A12	0.98	2.44	0.98	—	—	2961	0.960	0.00	0.13	0.13	—	0.96	3.3	0.0	WCA 3A	WCA 3A
SITE_62	P3	3A9	0.94	2.36	0.97	—	—	3017	0.943	0.00	0.17	0.16	—	0.94	4.1	0.0	WCA 3A	WCA 3A
SITE_62	P4	—	—	—	—	—	—	—	—	—	—	—	—	—	—	—	WCA 3A	—
SITE_63	P1	S11A_T	0.82	1.85	0.97	7.04	12.44	3080	0.947	0.00	0.22	0.22	10.061	0.95	4.1	0.0	WCA 3A	WCA 3A
SITE_63	P2	S142_H	0.82	3.10	0.97	—	—	2876	0.946	0.00	0.22	0.22	—	0.95	4.1	0.0	WCA 3A	L38E Canal
SITE_63	P3	S9A_T	0.90	2.54	0.98	—	—	2588	0.954	0.00	0.22	0.22	—	0.95	4.1	0.0	WCA 3A	WCA 3B
SITE_63	P4	—	—	—	—	—	—	—	—	—	—	—	—	—	—	—	WCA 3A	—
SITE_64	P1	W11	1.06	1.23	0.99	8.19	11.89	1849	0.977	0.00	0.12	0.12	10.063	0.98	3.3	0.0	WCA 3A	WCA 3A
SITE_64	P2	EDEN_8	1.03	1.62	0.98	—	—	803	0.966	0.00	0.11	0.11	—	0.98	3.0	0.0	WCA 3A	WCA 3A
SITE_64	P3	EDEN_12	0.77	3.69	0.98	—	—	784	0.964	0.00	0.11	0.11	—	0.97	3.1	0.0	WCA 3A	WCA 3A
SITE_64	P4	—	—	—	—	—	—	—	—	—	—	—	—	—	—	—	WCA 3A	—
SITE_65	P1	EDEN_8	0.88	2.36	0.99	7.83	11.15	801	0.990	-0.00	0.05	0.05	9.551	0.99	1.5	-0.0	WCA 3A	WCA 3A
SITE_65	P2	W5	0.95	1.93	0.99	—	—	1737	0.990	-0.00	0.07	0.07	—	0.99	2.2	-0.0	WCA 3A	WCA 3A
SITE_65	P3	W2	1.09	0.88	0.99	—	—	1781	0.982	-0.00	0.09	0.09	—	0.98	2.7	-0.0	WCA 3A	WCA 3A
SITE_65	P4	—	—	—	—	—	—	—	—	—	—	—	—	—	—	—	WCA 3A	—
SITE_69	P1	SITE_71	0.95	1.28	0.97	7.24	9.76	3119	0.945	0.00	0.10	0.10	8.629	0.94	4.1	0.0	WCA 3B	WCA 3B
SITE_69	P2	EDEN_12	0.40	5.35	0.98	—	—	787	0.955	0.00	0.07	0.07	—	0.96	2.7	0.0	WCA 3B	WCA 3A
SITE_69	P3	EDEN_8	0.54	4.26	0.98	—	—	806	0.954	0.00	0.07	0.07	—	0.96	2.7	0.0	WCA 3B	WCA 3A
SITE_69	P4	—	—	—	—	—	—	—	—	—	—	—	—	—	—	—	WCA 3B	—

Appendix 3. EDEN water-level estimation equations and performance statistics sorted by station name.—Continued

[n, number of data points; R², coefficient of determination; RMSE, root mean square error; WCA, Water Conservation Area; ENP, Everglades National Park; BCNP, Big Cypress National Preserve; FB, Florida Bay]

Station name	Predictor number	Predictor station name	Slope, m	y-intercept, b	Pearson correlation coefficient	Minimum observed	Maximum observed	n	R²	Mean error	RMSE	Standard error	Average measured, in feet	Nash-Sutcliffe	Percent model error	Percent model bias	Area of site	Area of predictor
SITE_7	P1	WCA1ME	0.98	1.86	0.99	14.88	17.57	3010	0.980	0.00	0.06	0.06	16.378	0.98	2.3	0.0	WCA 1	WCA 1
SITE_7	P2	SITE_9	0.85	2.55	0.96	—	—	3029	0.925	0.00	0.12	0.11	—	0.93	4.4	0.0	WCA 1	WCA 1
SITE_7	P3	SITE_8T	0.57	7.18	0.92	—	—	3030	0.848	-0.00	0.17	0.16	—	0.85	6.3	-0.0	WCA 1	WCA 1
SITE_7	P4	—	—	—	—	—	—	—	—	—	—	—	—	—	—	—	WCA 1	—
SITE_71	P1	TI-9	1.04	1.48	0.97	6.05	8.93	928	0.949	0.00	0.07	0.06	7.758	0.96	2.3	0.0	WCA 3B	WCA 3B
SITE_71	P2	SITE_69	1.00	-0.85	0.97	—	—	3119	0.945	-0.00	0.11	0.10	—	0.94	3.7	-0.0	WCA 3B	WCA 3B
SITE_71	P3	EDEN_7	0.69	3.59	0.96	—	—	791	0.928	-0.00	0.08	0.07	—	0.95	2.6	-0.0	WCA 3B	WCA 3B
SITE_71	P4	—	—	—	—	—	—	—	—	—	—	—	—	—	—	—	WCA 3B	—
SITE_76	P1	EDEN_7	0.87	2.34	0.96	5.41	8.79	764	0.914	0.00	0.11	0.10	7.580	0.93	3.1	0.0	WCA 3B	WCA 3B
SITE_76	P2	SITE_71	1.01	-0.27	0.95	—	—	3072	0.907	0.00	0.15	0.14	—	0.91	4.3	0.0	WCA 3B	WCA 3B
SITE_76	P3	SITE_69	1.00	-1.05	0.92	—	—	3104	0.854	-0.00	0.18	0.17	—	0.85	5.4	-0.0	WCA 3B	WCA 3B
SITE_76	P4	—	—	—	—	—	—	—	—	—	—	—	—	—	—	—	WCA 3B	—
SITE_8C	P1	S10C_H	1.00	0.14	1.00	12.09	17.63	3044	0.993	0.00	0.08	0.08	16.154	0.99	1.4	0.0	WCA 1	L39 Canal
SITE_8C	P2	S10D_H	1.01	-0.01	1.00	—	—	3036	0.992	0.00	0.08	0.08	—	0.99	1.4	0.0	WCA 1	L39 Canal
SITE_8C	P3	S10A_H	1.00	0.21	1.00	—	—	3014	0.991	0.00	0.08	0.08	—	0.99	1.5	0.0	WCA 1	L39 Canal
SITE_8C	P4	—	—	—	—	—	—	—	—	—	—	—	—	—	—	—	WCA 1	—
SITE_8T	P1	SITE_8C	0.77	3.66	0.98	13.93	17.47	3028	0.951	0.00	0.16	0.15	16.139	0.95	4.4	0.0	WCA 1	WCA 1
SITE_8T	P2	S10D_H	0.80	3.24	0.98	—	—	3096	0.951	0.00	0.15	0.15	—	0.95	4.4	0.0	WCA 1	L39 Canal
SITE_8T	P3	S10C_H	0.77	3.79	0.97	—	—	3104	0.936	0.00	0.18	0.17	—	0.94	5.0	0.0	WCA 1	L39 Canal
SITE_8T	P4	—	—	—	—	—	—	—	—	—	—	—	—	—	—	—	WCA 1	—
SITE_9	P1	WCA1ME	1.09	0.04	0.98	14.78	17.43	3095	0.957	-0.00	0.10	0.10	16.260	0.96	3.9	-0.0	WCA 1	WCA 1
SITE_9	P2	SITE_8T	0.68	5.32	0.97	—	—	3101	0.934	-0.00	0.13	0.12	—	0.93	4.8	-0.0	WCA 1	WCA 1
SITE_9	P3	SITE_7	1.09	-1.56	0.96	—	—	3029	0.925	-0.00	0.13	0.13	—	0.93	5.1	-0.0	WCA 1	WCA 1
SITE_9	P4	—	—	—	—	—	—	—	—	—	—	—	—	—	—	—	WCA 1	—
SITE_99	P1	EDEN_13	1.53	-2.89	0.87	4.37	11.39	740	0.761	-0.00	0.52	0.46	9.640	0.80	7.4	-0.0	WCA 2B	WCA 2B
SITE_99	P2	S150_T	0.72	3.52	0.83	—	—	1200	0.600	-0.04	0.61	0.52	—	0.60	8.7	-0.4	WCA 2B	WCA 3A
SITE_99	P3	EDEN_12	1.58	-3.41	0.83	—	—	787	0.682	-0.00	0.83	0.69	—	0.75	11.8	-0.0	WCA 2B	WCA 3A
SITE_99	P4	—	—	—	—	—	—	—	—	—	—	—	—	—	—	—	WCA 2B	—
SOUTH_CA1	P1	NORTH_CA1	0.97	-0.07	0.91	12.88	17.27	2555	0.826	-0.00	0.41	0.37	15.317	0.83	9.3	-0.0	WCA 1	WCA 1
SOUTH_CA1	P2	EDEN_13	0.85	8.09	0.84	—	—	745	0.701	-0.00	0.34	0.28	—	0.83	7.7	-0.0	WCA 1	WCA 2B
SOUTH_CA1	P3	EDEN_8	1.01	6.70	0.81	—	—	806	0.651	-0.00	0.43	0.35	—	0.81	9.7	-0.0	WCA 1	WCA 3A
SOUTH_CA1	P4	—	—	—	—	—	—	—	—	—	—	—	—	—	—	—	WCA 1	—

Appendix 3. EDEN water-level estimation equations and performance statistics sorted by station name.—Continued

[n, number of data points; R², coefficient of determination; RMSE, root mean square error; WCA, Water Conservation Area; ENP, Everglades National Park; BCNP, Big Cypress National Preserve; FB, Florida Bay]

Station name	Predictor number[a]	Predictor station name	Slope, m	y-intercept, b	Pearson correlation coefficient	Minimum observed[a]	Maximum observed[a]	n	R²	Mean error	RMSE	Standard error	Average measured, in feet[a]	Nash-Sutcliffe	Percent model error	Percent model bias	Area of site	Area of predictor
SP	P1	DO2	0.74	-0.36	0.95	-2.25	2.74	3096	0.910	0.00	0.23	0.22	0.545	0.91	4.6	0.0	ENP	ENP
SP	P2	CY3	0.92	0.10	0.95	—	—	3096	0.900	0.00	0.24	0.23	—	0.90	4.9	0.0	ENP	ENP
SP	P3	NP46	1.05	0.66	0.94	—	—	3084	0.903	-0.01	0.24	0.22	—	0.90	4.8	-1.6	ENP	ENP
SP	P4	—	—	—	—	—	—	—	—	—	—	—	—	—	—	—	ENP	—
SRS1	P1	TI-8	1.09	1.30	0.98	5.23	8.81	941	0.964	-0.00	0.09	0.09	7.419	0.97	2.4	-0.0	WCA 3B	WCA 3B
SRS1	P2	3BS1W1	0.66	4.07	0.98	—	—	2799	0.951	0.00	0.13	0.12	—	0.95	3.6	0.0	WCA 3B	WCA 3B
SRS1	P3	EDEN_10	1.26	-0.10	0.97	—	—	801	0.936	0.00	0.12	0.11	—	0.95	3.3	0.0	WCA 3B	WCA 3B
SRS1	P4	—	—	—	—	—	—	—	—	—	—	—	—	—	—	—	WCA 3B	—
Stillwater_Creek	P1	West_High-way_Creek	0.98	-0.07	0.99	-1.56	1.42	3108	0.985	-0.00	0.04	0.04	-0.708	0.98	1.4	0.0	Coast of FB	Coast of FB
Stillwater_Creek	P2	Upstream_Taylor_River	0.73	-0.44	0.89	—	—	3040	0.793	-0.00	0.15	0.14	—	0.79	5.1	0.0	Coast of FB	Coast of FB
Stillwater_Creek	P3	Joe_Bay_2E	0.74	-0.35	0.88	—	—	1359	0.779	0.00	0.16	0.14	—	0.78	5.4	-0.1	Coast of FB	Coast of FB
Stillwater_Creek	P4	—	—	—	—	—	—	—	—	—	—	—	—	—	—	—	Coast of FB	—
Taylor_River_at_mouth	P1	Mud_Creek_at_mouth	0.96	-0.03	0.99	-1.66	2.47	3075	0.979	-0.00	0.05	0.05	-0.609	0.98	1.2	0.0	Coast of FB	Coast of FB
Taylor_River_at_mouth	P2	Trout_Creek_at_mouth	0.93	-0.07	0.97	—	—	3135	0.947	-0.00	0.08	0.08	—	0.95	2.0	0.0	Coast of FB	Coast of FB
Taylor_River_at_mouth	P3	McCor-mick_Creek_at_mouth	0.89	-0.12	0.95	—	—	3128	0.908	-0.00	0.11	0.10	—	0.91	2.6	0.0	Coast of FB	Coast of FB
Taylor_River_at_mouth	P4	—	—	—	—	—	—	—	—	—	—	—	—	—	—	—	Coast of FB	—

Appendix 3.   EDEN water-level estimation equations and performance statistics sorted by station name.—Continued

[n, number of data points; R², coefficient of determination; RMSE, root mean square error; WCA, Water Conservation Area; ENP, Everglades National Park; BCNP, Big Cypress National Preserve; FB, Florida Bay]

[a]Station name	[a]Predictor number	Predictor station name	Slope, m	y-intercept, b	Pearson correlation coefficient	[a]Minimum observed	[a]Maximum observed	n	R²	Mean error	RMSE	Standard error	[a]Average measured, in feet	Nash-Sutcliffe	Percent model error	Percent model bias	Area of site	Area of predictor
Taylor_Slough_wetland_at_E146	P1	E146	1.04	0.10	0.99	-0.72	1.42	1030	0.989	0.00	0.04	0.04	-0.007	0.99	1.7	-1.6	ENP	ENP
Taylor_Slough_wetland_at_E146	P2	P37	0.95	-0.22	0.98	—	—	1030	0.961	0.00	0.07	0.07	—	0.96	3.3	-3.4	ENP	ENP
Taylor_Slough_wetland_at_E146	P3	NCL	0.88	-0.09	0.97	—	—	968	0.953	0.00	0.08	0.08	—	0.95	3.5	-38.3	ENP	ENP
Taylor_Slough_wetland_at_E146	P4	—	—	—	—	—	—	—	—	—	—	—	—	—	—	—	ENP	—
TI-8	P1	SRS1	0.89	-0.96	0.98	4.42	6.21	941	0.964	0.00	0.08	0.08	5.352	0.96	4.4	0.0	WCA 3B	WCA 3B
TI-8	P2	EDEN_10	1.14	-1.16	0.97	—	—	801	0.936	0.00	0.11	0.10	—	0.94	5.9	0.0	WCA 3B	WCA 3B
TI-8	P3	3BS1W1	0.54	2.84	0.97	—	—	858	0.935	0.00	0.11	0.11	—	0.93	6.1	0.0	WCA 3B	WCA 3B
TI-8	P4	—	—	—	—	—	—	—	—	—	—	—	—	—	—	—	WCA 3B	—
TI-9	P1	SITE_71	0.91	-1.04	0.97	5.06	6.54	928	0.949	-0.00	0.06	0.06	5.864	0.95	4.2	-0.0	WCA 3B	WCA 3B
TI-9	P2	TI-8	0.62	2.53	0.95	—	—	941	0.903	-0.00	0.08	0.08	—	0.90	5.7	-0.0	WCA 3B	WCA 3B
TI-9	P3	SITE_69	0.79	-0.88	0.95	—	—	941	0.900	-0.00	0.09	0.08	—	0.90	5.8	-0.0	WCA 3B	WCA 3B
TI-9	P4	—	—	—	—	—	—	—	—	—	—	—	—	—	—	—	WCA 3B	—
TMC	P1	TSB	0.66	1.58	0.83	-0.83	4.36	1799	0.683	-0.00	0.51	0.42	2.702	0.69	9.8	-0.0	ENP	ENP
TMC	P2	RG1	0.89	-0.89	0.82	—	—	3127	0.761	0.04	0.49	0.45	—	0.76	9.4	1.6	ENP	ENP
TMC	P3	NP206	0.90	-0.93	0.81	—	—	3155	0.756	0.04	0.49	0.45	—	0.75	9.5	1.6	ENP	ENP
TMC	P4	—	—	—	—	—	—	—	—	—	—	—	—	—	—	—	ENP	—

Appendix 3.   EDEN water-level estimation equations and performance statistics sorted by station name.—Continued

[n, number of data points; R², coefficient of determination; RMSE, root mean square error; WCA, Water Conservation Area; ENP, Everglades National Park; BCNP, Big Cypress National Preserve; FB, Florida Bay]

[a]Station name	[a]Predictor number	Predictor station name	Slope, m	y-intercept, b	Pearson correlation coefficient	[a]Minimum observed	[a]Maximum observed	n	R²	Mean error	RMSE	Standard error	[a]Average measured, in feet	Nash-Sutcliffe	Percent model error	Percent model bias	Area of site	Area of predictor
Trout_Creek_at_mouth	P1	Mud_Creek_at_mouth	1.01	0.02	0.99	-1.62	1.71	3057	0.976	0.00	0.06	0.06	-0.586	0.98	1.7	-0.0	Coast of FB	Coast of FB
Trout_Creek_at_mouth	P2	Taylor_River_at_mouth	1.02	0.04	0.97	—	—	3135	0.947	0.00	0.08	0.08	—	0.95	2.5	-0.0	Coast of FB	Coast of FB
Trout_Creek_at_mouth	P3	McCormick_Creek_at_mouth	0.95	-0.07	0.97	—	—	3110	0.946	0.00	0.09	0.08	—	0.95	2.6	-0.0	Coast of FB	Coast of FB
Trout_Creek_at_mouth	P4	—	—	—	—	—	—	—	—	—	—	—	—	—	—	—	Coast of FB	—
TSB	P1	E112	1.00	-0.75	0.99	-1.04	4.04	1799	0.979	-0.00	0.16	0.16	1.872	0.98	3.2	-0.0	ENP	ENP
TSB	P2	NTS1	0.99	-0.95	0.98	—	—	1799	0.953	0.00	0.25	0.24	—	0.95	4.8	0.0	ENP	ENP
TSB	P3	S175_T	1.86	0.08	0.97	—	—	1787	0.934	0.00	0.29	0.28	—	0.93	5.7	0.0	ENP	L31W Canal
TSB	P4	—	—	—	—	—	—	—	—	—	—	—	—	—	—	—	ENP	—
TSH	P1	R127	0.85	-0.17	0.98	-1.76	1.81	3138	0.975	0.00	0.09	0.09	0.374	0.97	2.6	0.6	ENP	ENP
TSH	P2	P37	0.95	0.49	0.97	—	—	3155	0.946	-0.00	0.14	0.13	—	0.95	3.8	-0.0	ENP	ENP
TSH	P3	NP67	0.85	-0.09	0.96	—	—	3116	0.942	-0.00	0.14	0.14	—	0.94	4.0	-0.9	ENP	ENP
TSH	P4	—	—	—	—	—	—	—	—	—	—	—	—	—	—	—	ENP	—
Upstream_Taylor_River	P1	Joe_Bay_2E	0.97	0.11	0.96	-1.29	1.39	1329	0.913	0.00	0.12	0.11	-0.367	0.91	4.5	-0.1	Coast of FB	Coast of FB
Upstream_Taylor_River	P2	McCormick_Creek_at_mouth	0.99	0.18	0.91	—	—	3050	0.823	0.00	0.17	0.16	—	0.82	6.4	-0.0	Coast of FB	Coast of FB
Upstream_Taylor_River	P3	Stillwater_Creek	1.08	0.40	0.89	—	—	3040	0.793	0.00	0.19	0.16	—	0.79	6.9	-0.0	Coast of FB	Coast of FB
Upstream_Taylor_River	P4	—	—	—	—	—	—	—	—	—	—	—	—	—	—	—	Coast of FB	—
W11	P1	SITE_64	0.92	-0.94	0.99	6.95	10.14	1849	0.977	-0.00	0.11	0.11	8.339	0.98	3.5	-0.0	WCA 3A	WCA 3A
W11	P2	W18	1.00	-0.22	0.98	—	—	1539	0.954	-0.00	0.15	0.15	—	0.95	4.7	-0.0	WCA 3A	WCA 3A
W11	P3	SITE_69	1.70	-6.39	0.97	—	—	1864	0.949	-0.00	0.17	0.16	—	0.95	5.3	-0.0	WCA 3A	WCA 3B
W11	P4	—	—	—	—	—	—	—	—	—	—	—	—	—	—	—	WCA 3A	—

Appendix 3. EDEN water-level estimation equations and performance statistics sorted by station name.—Continued

[n, number of data points; R², coefficient of determination; RMSE, root mean square error; WCA, Water Conservation Area; ENP, Everglades National Park; BCNP, Big Cypress National Preserve; FB, Florida Bay]

Station name	Predictor number	Predictor station name	Slope, m	y-intercept, b	Pearson correlation coefficient	Minimum observed	Maximum observed	n	R²	Mean error	RMSE	Standard error	Average measured, in feet	Nash-Sutcliffe	Percent model error	Percent model bias	Area of site	Area of predictor
W14	P1	EDEN_8	1.04	-0.31	0.99	6.14	10.02	728	0.974	0.00	0.09	0.09	8.093	0.98	2.2	0.0	WCA 3A	WCA 3A
W14	P2	EDEN_12	0.78	1.80	0.98	—	—	708	0.965	0.00	0.10	0.10	—	0.97	2.6	0.0	WCA 3A	WCA 3A
W14	P3	W5	1.10	-0.67	0.98	—	—	1678	0.956	0.00	0.17	0.17	—	0.96	4.4	0.0	WCA 3A	WCA 3A
W14	P4	—	—	—	—	—	—	—	—	—	—	—	—	—	—	—	WCA 3A	—
W15	P1	W11	0.94	0.50	0.97	7.47	9.67	808	0.937	0.00	0.12	0.11	8.178	0.94	5.4	0.0	WCA 3A	WCA 3A
W15	P2	3A-5	1.07	-1.18	0.97	—	—	697	0.933	-0.00	0.12	0.12	—	0.93	5.6	-0.0	WCA 3A	WCA 3A
W15	P3	W18	1.02	-0.37	0.96	—	—	757	0.914	-0.00	0.14	0.13	—	0.91	6.1	-0.0	WCA 3A	WCA 3A
W15	P4	—	—	—	—	—	—	—	—	—	—	—	—	—	—	—	WCA 3A	—
W18	P1	W11	0.95	0.60	0.98	7.24	10.35	1539	0.954	0.00	0.15	0.14	8.622	0.95	4.7	0.0	WCA 3A	WCA 3A
W18	P2	EDEN_14	0.98	-0.13	0.97	—	—	647	0.950	-0.00	0.10	0.10	—	0.95	3.2	-0.0	WCA 3A	WCA 3A
W18	P3	3A-5	1.04	-0.65	0.97	—	—	663	0.946	0.00	0.11	0.11	—	0.95	3.6	0.0	WCA 3A	WCA 3A
W18	P4	—	—	—	—	—	—	—	—	—	—	—	—	—	—	—	WCA 3A	—
W2	P1	W5	0.87	1.04	0.99	6.65	9.53	1590	0.987	-0.00	0.07	0.07	8.027	0.99	2.5	-0.0	WCA 3A	WCA 3A
W2	P2	SITE_65	0.90	-0.65	0.99	—	—	1781	0.982	0.00	0.08	0.08	—	0.98	2.9	0.0	WCA 3A	WCA 3A
W2	P3	S12D_H	0.83	0.08	0.99	—	—	1775	0.972	-0.00	0.10	0.10	—	0.97	3.6	-0.0	WCA 3A	Tamiami Canal
W2	P4	—	—	—	—	—	—	—	—	—	—	—	—	—	—	—	WCA 3A	—
W5	P1	SITE_65	1.04	-1.92	0.99	6.64	9.65	1737	0.990	0.00	0.07	0.07	7.999	0.99	2.5	0.0	WCA 3A	WCA 3A
W5	P2	W2	1.14	-1.07	0.99	—	—	1590	0.987	0.00	0.08	0.08	—	0.99	2.7	0.0	WCA 3A	WCA 3A
W5	P3	EDEN_8	0.92	0.52	0.99	—	—	785	0.982	0.00	0.07	0.07	—	0.99	2.3	0.0	WCA 3A	WCA 3A
W5	P4	—	—	—	—	—	—	—	—	—	—	—	—	—	—	—	WCA 3A	—
WCA1ME	P1	SITE_7	1.00	-1.56	0.99	13.39	15.96	3010	0.980	-0.00	0.06	0.06	14.849	0.98	2.4	-0.0	WCA 1	WCA 1
WCA1ME	P2	SITE_9	0.88	0.59	0.98	—	—	3095	0.957	0.00	0.09	0.09	—	0.96	3.6	0.0	WCA 1	WCA 1
WCA1ME	P3	SITE_8T	0.60	5.24	0.95	—	—	3083	0.893	0.00	0.15	0.14	—	0.89	5.7	0.0	WCA 1	WCA 1
WCA1ME	P4	—	—	—	—	—	—	—	—	—	—	—	—	—	—	—	WCA 1	—
WCA2E1	P1	S10A_T	0.76	1.42	0.90	9.64	14.32	2839	0.804	0.00	0.30	0.27	11.234	0.80	6.5	0.0	WCA 2A	WCA 2A
WCA2E1	P2	SITE_17	0.77	1.85	0.89	—	—	2873	0.794	0.00	0.31	0.28	—	0.79	6.7	0.0	WCA 2A	WCA 2A
WCA2E1	P3	SITE_19	0.70	2.74	0.89	—	—	2864	0.793	0.00	0.31	0.28	—	0.79	6.6	0.0	WCA 2A	WCA 2A
WCA2E1	P4	—	—	—	—	—	—	—	—	—	—	—	—	—	—	—	WCA 2A	—
WCA2E4	P1	SITE_19	0.77	1.56	0.97	10.19	13.35	2457	0.943	0.00	0.16	0.16	10.981	0.94	5.2	0.0	WCA 2A	WCA 2A
WCA2E4	P2	SITE_17	0.82	0.86	0.96	—	—	2467	0.925	0.00	0.19	0.18	—	0.92	5.9	0.0	WCA 2A	WCA 2A
WCA2E4	P3	S145_H	0.61	4.69	0.91	—	—	2276	0.821	0.00	0.28	0.25	—	0.82	8.8	0.0	WCA 2A	WCA 2A
WCA2E4	P4	—	—	—	—	—	—	—	—	—	—	—	—	—	—	—	WCA 2A	—
WCA2F1	P1	SITE_17	0.79	1.67	0.90	9.87	14.45	2808	0.801	0.00	0.32	0.28	11.338	0.80	6.9	0.0	WCA 2A	WCA 2A
WCA2F1	P2	SITE_19	0.70	2.82	0.89	—	—	2762	0.785	0.00	0.32	0.28	—	0.79	7.0	0.0	WCA 2A	WCA 2A
WCA2F1	P3	S10A_T	0.75	1.59	0.88	—	—	2776	0.771	0.00	0.34	0.30	—	0.77	7.4	0.0	WCA 2A	WCA 2A
WCA2F1	P4	—	—	—	—	—	—	—	—	—	—	—	—	—	—	—	WCA 2A	—

Appendix 3. EDEN water-level estimation equations and performance statistics sorted by station name.—Continued

[n, number of data points; R^2, coefficient of determination; RMSE, root mean square error; WCA, Water Conservation Area; ENP, Everglades National Park; BCNP, Big Cypress National Preserve; FB, Florida Bay]

[a]Station name	[a]Predictor number	Predictor station name	Slope, m	y-intercept, b	Pearson correlation coefficient	[a]Minimum observed	[a]Maximum observed	n	R^2	Mean error	RMSE	Standard error	[a]Average measured, in feet	Nash-Sutcliffe	Percent model error	Percent model bias	Area of site	Area of predictor
WCA2F4	P1	SITE_17	0.85	0.60	0.98	10.10	13.39	2475	0.951	0.00	0.15	0.15	11.017	0.95	4.6	0.0	WCA 2A	WCA 2A
WCA2F4	P2	SITE_19	0.76	1.76	0.97	—	—	2501	0.937	0.00	0.17	0.17	—	0.94	5.2	0.0	WCA 2A	WCA 2A
WCA2F4	P3	S145_H	0.63	4.57	0.92	—	—	2277	0.837	0.00	0.27	0.25	—	0.84	8.1	0.0	WCA 2A	WCA 2A
WCA2F4	P4	—	—	—	—	—	—	—	—	—	—	—	—	—	—	—	WCA 2A	—
WCA2RT	[b]P1	S7_T	0.61	3.08	0.94	8.42	12.18	2548	0.892	0.00	0.26	0.25	9.686	0.89	7.0	0.0	WCA 2A	L38E Canal
WCA2RT	[b]P2	EDEN_11	1.39	-6.20	0.93	—	—	621	0.881	0.00	0.26	0.24	—	0.88	6.8	0.0	WCA 2A	WCA 2A
WCA2RT	[b]P3	SITE_17	0.91	-1.50	0.90	—	—	2529	0.803	0.01	0.36	0.32	—	0.80	9.5	0.1	WCA 2A	WCA 2A
WCA2RT	[b]P4	—	—	—	—	—	—	—	—	—	—	—	—	—	—	—	WCA 2A	—
WCA2RT	[c]P1	S7_T	0.61	3.08	0.98	—	—	—	—	—	—	—	—	—	—	—	WCA 2A	L38E Canal
WCA2RT	[c]P2	EDEN_11	1.39	-6.20	0.99	—	—	—	—	—	—	—	—	—	—	—	WCA 2A	WCA 2A
WCA2RT	[c]P3	SITE_17	0.91	-1.50	0.99	—	—	—	—	—	—	—	—	—	—	—	WCA 2A	WCA 2A
WCA2RT	[c]P4	—	—	—	—	—	—	—	—	—	—	—	—	—	—	—	WCA 2A	—
WCA2U1	P1	S146_H	0.90	1.66	0.99	9.34	12.83	1970	0.976	0.00	0.12	0.12	10.494	0.98	3.5	0.0	WCA 2A	WCA 2A
WCA2U1	P2	S145_H	0.89	1.39	0.98	—	—	2176	0.953	-0.01	0.17	0.17	—	0.95	5.0	-0.1	WCA 2A	WCA 2A
WCA2U1	P3	SITE_19	1.02	-1.83	0.98	—	—	2407	0.961	-0.00	0.16	0.16	—	0.96	4.5	-0.0	WCA 2A	WCA 2A
WCA2U1	P4	—	—	—	—	—	—	—	—	—	—	—	—	—	—	—	WCA 2A	—
WCA2U3	P1	SITE_17	0.99	-1.42	1.00	8.97	13.11	2690	0.999	0.00	0.02	0.02	10.751	1.00	0.5	0.0	WCA 2A	WCA 2A
WCA2U3	P2	SITE_19	0.88	0.06	0.98	—	—	2645	0.959	-0.01	0.16	0.16	—	0.96	3.9	-0.1	WCA 2A	WCA 2A
WCA2U3	P3	S146_H	0.77	3.19	0.97	—	—	2126	0.932	0.01	0.20	0.19	—	0.93	4.8	0.1	WCA 2A	WCA 2A
WCA2U3	P4	—	—	—	—	—	—	—	—	—	—	—	—	—	—	—	WCA 2A	—
West_Highway_Creek	P1	Stillwater_Creek	1.01	0.06	0.99	-1.42	1.60	3108	0.985	0.00	0.04	0.04	-0.655	0.98	1.4	-0.0	Coast of FB	Coast of FB
West_Highway_Creek	P2	Joe_Bay_2E	0.75	-0.28	0.89	—	—	1358	0.788	0.00	0.16	0.14	—	0.79	5.3	-0.1	Coast of FB	Coast of FB
West_Highway_Creek	P3	Taylor_River_at_mouth	0.87	-0.12	0.89	—	—	3150	0.786	0.00	0.16	0.14	—	0.79	5.3	-0.0	Coast of FB	Coast of FB
West_Highway_Creek	P4	—	—	—	—	—	—	—	—	—	—	—	—	—	—	—	Coast of FB	—

[a] Datum of data as stored in the National Water Information System. See appendixes 1 and 2 for a listing. Data for predictors must use the datum listed in appendixes 1 and 2. The water-level estimation will be for the datum used for the gage.

[b] Datum change at the gage on 12/10/2008. Equations are only valid to this date.

[c] New datum for gage on 12/11/2008. Equations developed using data from 12/11–31/2008. Statistics were not generated on the limited dataset.